RALPH
VAUGHAN
WILLIAMS

CLASSIC *f*M
LIFELINES

V RALPH
AUGHAN
WILLIAMS

AN ESSENTIAL GUIDE
TO HIS LIFE AND WORKS

MICHAEL JAMESON

PAVILION

First published in Great Britain in 1997 by
PAVILION BOOKS LIMITED
26 Upper Ground, London SE1 9PD

Copyright © Pavilion Books Ltd 1997
Front cover illustration © The Lebrecht Collection

Edited and designed by Castle House Press, Penarth, South Wales
Cover designed by Bet Ayer

A CIP catalogue record for this book is available
from the British Library

ISBN 1 86205 021 X

Set in Lydian and Caslon
Printed and bound in Great Britain by Mackays of Chatham

2 4 6 8 10 9 7 5 3 1

This book can be ordered direct from the publisher.
Please contact the Marketing Department.
But try your bookshop first.

ACKNOWLEDGMENTS

The one person who would have taken greatest delight in seeing this volume come to fruition is sadly not with us to witness the event. But in so many ways, my mum, to whom this little book is dedicated with love, is still very much a part of our lives, and always will be. Her faith, her fun, her determination, her care and compassion for others and, at the end, her courage in the face of tragedy, exemplified goodness and truth. You gave me the best possible example to live by, and showed me how to live my life aright.

Special thanks to Bob Cowan, who originally saw to it that my name got mentioned in despatches, and without whose timely intervention this publication would almost certainly have appeared with someone else's name on the cover. Finally, a big thank-you to all at Castle House Press, and principally to Eileen Townsend Jones, whose guidance, patience, and expertise has kept my unruly text in order.

As Mr. Heifetz would say at the conclusion of a violin recital:

To those that liked it . . . thanks.
To those that didn't . . . maybe we'll catch you the next time!

Michael Jameson
Southampton, February 1997

Contents

A NOTE FROM THE EDITORS

A biography of this type inevitably contains numerous references to pieces of music. The paragraphs are also peppered with 'quotation marks', since much of the tale is told through reported speech.

Because of this, and to make things more accessible for the reader as well as easier on the eye, we decided to simplify the method of typesetting the names of musical works. Conventionally this is determined by the nature of the individual work, following a set of rules whereby some pieces appear in italics, some in italics and quotation marks, others in plain roman type and others still in roman and quotation marks.

In this book, the names of all musical works are simply set in italics. Songs and arias appear in italics and quotation marks.

CHAPTER 1
FROM TINY ACORNS
(1872–90)

- ♦ *Family background*
- ♦ *The Darwin connection*
- ♦ *Enter the Wedgwoods*
- ♦ *Vaughan Williams's parents*
- ♦ *Ralph's birth*
- ♦ *Earliest musical experiences*

Writing in his 1953 essay *A Musical Autobiography*, Ralph Vaughan Williams recalled: 'When I was about six I wrote a pianoforte piece, four bars long, called, heaven knows why, *The Robin's Nest*. . . .' By the time he recounted these first uncertain steps upon the road to musical greatness, he had long been the undisputed elder statesman of British music, and was universally acknowledged as the finest symphonic composer England had produced since Elgar. Redoubtable, corpulent and imposing in later life, Vaughan Williams nevertheless wore worldly fame with touching modesty, and a ready wit which often bespoke humility born of a recognition that, in the customary human scheme of things, only seldom do tiny acorns grow into mighty musical oaks.

But if heredity does indeed predispose men to great endeavour, heroism, or genius, Ralph Vaughan Williams had more to be thankful for than most. His grandfather, great-grandfather, and at least one of his uncles, had risen to the highest echelons of the English judiciary, while his mother was both niece of Charles Darwin, author of *The Origin of Species*, and a direct descendant of Staffordshire pottery magnate Josiah Wedgwood.

The paternal line was of Welsh extraction. John Williams,

born at Job's Well near Carmarthen in 1757, read law at Jesus College, Oxford, becoming a fellow of Wadham College in 1780, and Serjeant-at-Law in 1794. His obituary (recorded in the Annual Register for 1810) paid tribute to his 'extraordinary powers of memory, excellent understanding, patient and persevering application to the study of law, and luminous expositions, sound deductions, and clear reasoning.' His second son, Edward Vaughan Williams (the composer's grandfather), was born in 1797, and educated at Winchester College and Westminster School, and subsequently won a scholarship to read law at Trinity College, Cambridge, in 1816.

Edward's legal career rapidly eclipsed his father's in distinction, both at the bar, and as author of such weighty legal treatises as *On the Law of Executors and Administrators*, which ran into seven editions before its author's retirement from the bench in 1865. Sir Edward received his knighthood in 1847, and statistics endorse his profound common sense and virtually infallible judgement, as fewer re-trials are recorded in cases heard by him than by any of his contemporaries. Unexpectedly diffident in manner, he was, nonetheless, a man of punctilious habits, and although his depositions were famously short, accurate, and concise, his obituary noted that his 'choice of words was fastidious, though his delivery somewhat laboured and embarrassed.'

In 1828, Sir Edward Vaughan Williams had married Jane Bagot (reputedly a descendant of the eponymous 'creature of Richard II' of Shakespearian notoriety), and their union produced six sons and a single daughter. The boys were educated at Westminster, and spent holidays at the family's rented house, Tanhurst, which nestled on the southern slopes of Leith Hill, and afforded magnificent views of the South Downs. Edward and Arthur, born in 1833 and 1834, the second and third sons, both entered the Church. The first, Hervey, had died at twenty-three. Lewis, born in 1836, had joined the Brigade of Rifles, and also died young, whilst Roland and Walter continued the family legal tradition.

Arthur Charles Vaughan Williams matriculated at Christ Church, Oxford, in June 1853, and took his B.A. four years later. In 1860 he was ordained as a deacon, and took up his first clerical appointment as curate in George Herbert's former parish of Bemerton, near Salisbury. It was a happy and productive time;

the Vicar of Bemerton, the Revd. Wellesley Pole Pigott wrote to Sir Edward expressing both gratitude and remorse as Arthur left his parish for a new living at Halsall, near Ormskirk, in 1863:

It was quite affecting to see the school children on Sunday in tears at his leaving, and I can assure you they were not the only ones . . . we have worked together in perfect harmony during the time he has been here. I trust that his ministry may prove a lasting blessing to the parish.

Arthur took Holy Orders and entered the Priesthood in 1865, whereupon he was dispatched south once again, to the Parish of Alverstoke in Hampshire. Now more conveniently situated, he became a regular visitor to the family home, Tanhurst, and became acquainted with the household's nearest neighbours, who lived in a splendid, if much extended house, Leith Hill Place, originally constructed at the end of the seventeenth century. In 1847, the property, together with its adjoining farm, had been purchased by Josiah Wedgwood II (grandson of the illustrious founder of the family pottery firm), who was then in his fifty-second year, having married his cousin Caroline Darwin a decade previously. The couple now had three young daughters (a fourth had died in infancy) who could now enjoy the delights of the place, with its expansive vistas over both the Surrey Downs and Sussex Weald.

The wooded tract between Tanhurst and Leith Hill Place, burgeoning in season with azaleas and rhododendrons planted by the Wedgwoods, was an exotic and surprising place, the more eventful for sporadic glimpses of the kangaroos that the Evelyn family, Lords of the Manor, had established there. It was a vision of Albion itself, and it was here that the three girls, Sophy, Margaret, and Lucy, were periodically enlisted by their uncle, Charles Darwin, to assist with experiments in botany and zoology. Lucy and Sophy worked tirelessly, with knitting-needle and magnifying glass in hand, probing below the lawns and flower beds into the crepuscular world of the earthworm. Margaret, meanwhile, preferred to sketch her observations, while Sophy's early musical promise did not go unnoticed. The trio were not conventionally beautifully perhaps, but each possessed strong features, enquiring minds, and what Ursula Vaughan Williams (the composer's second wife, whom he would marry in 1953) has termed 'an air of distinction, and the poise that comes from unquestioned security.'

When asked just why Sir Edward Vaughan Williams had chosen to settle in the district, his riposte (delivered with the sagacity and verbal economy for which he was noted) could not have been more succinct: 'because it is full of charming young heiresses.' A close bond of friendship and mutual respect existed between the Leith Hill Place and Tanhurst households, and it probably came as a surprise to no one when the engagement of Arthur Vaughan Williams and Miss Margaret Wedgwood was announced in September 1867.

Indeed, no prospective match could have given greater satisfaction to the respective families, as Lady Vaughan Williams wrote to her son:

> *No piece of news could have made me so happy and I am sure I may use the same words as regards your papa. We had been for a long time hoping we might some day see Margaret Wedgwood your wife – and now the wished-for tidings have come, we are made still happier by hearing that both Mr and Mrs Wedgwood so cordially approve the engagement, and that they and their girls have expressed themselves so kindly about it. . . .*

Josiah Wedgwood, with characteristic entrepreneurial prudence, struck a more sanguine note, writing to his future son-in-law in the following terms:

> *If you can make up your minds to a small income at first, I see no objection to the marriage taking place as soon as you can be released from the Rev. Walpole. . . I propose allowing Margaret £500 a year, and ultimately she will have one third of my property, which latterly has yielded about £4,000 a year. The amount is uncertain, because it depends almost entirely on railroads. . . .*

Margaret, meanwhile, wrote daily to her fiancé, the correspondence detailing both her anxieties over his frequent colds, and her own efforts to master the culinary and domestic arts that were the metier of every dutiful Victorian wife; a large exercise book contains her earliest recipes for soup and milk puddings.

By Christmas, Arthur's commitments to the parishioners of Alverstoke were ended. Early in the New Year, he had accepted a new living at Down Ampney, on the borders of Wiltshire and Gloucestershire, and was at last free to marry. On 22 February 1868, Arthur and Margaret were united in matrimony at Coldharbour Church, and, shortly afterwards, settled into the vicarage at Down Ampney. Of the couple's three children, only the eldest, Hervey, was not born there. Margaret (Meggie) and Ralph were born at Down Ampney Vicarage, Ralph on Saturday 12 October 1872. Their father would remain at the vicarage until his death on 9 February 1875.

For a 'Saturday's Child', whom the old adage suggests 'has far to go', Ralph's passage through this life very nearly met an untimely and premature end, when the minister taking his christening service lost his grip of the child at the font; disaster was only narrowly averted when his ever-watchful mother managed to grab the baby's christening robe. Ralph's early years (his Christian name, incidentally, is pronounced 'Rafe', as he was quick to point out to those in error) were uneventful. After the death of her husband, Margaret and the children returned to live with her sister Sophy at Leith Hill Place.

As well as providing an inspirational location (on a clear day, one could easily see the twin windmills of Hassocks, Sussex, over twenty miles distant), Leith Hill Place itself played a part in nurturing the artistic sensibilities of its inhabitants. Its walls bore many fine portraits, some by Sir Joshua Reynolds and George Stubbs, mainly Wedgwood family commissions, although in other respects it was a drab, conventionally furnished home, in which virtue was taught by example, and discipline was strictly applied. Ralph, who had learned to read at his grandmother's knee, with the help of such volumes as the 1837 edition of *Cobwebs to Catch Flies* – a tutor advocated by Erasmus Darwin in his *Plan for the Conduct of Female Education in Board Schools* (1797) – gained his first literary insights from the very books once used by the young Charles Darwin; perhaps it was he who had painted its woodcut illustrations so meticulously in bright watercolour tints.

Vaughan Williams's humorous recollections of his earliest music lessons recount his early efforts under the watchful guidance of his Aunt Sophy. His childish four-bar melody *The Robin's Nest* was shown to some musical visitors:

My sister heard one of them say, 'Has he learnt any thoroughbass?'
We pondered for long over what 'thoroughbass' could be. Of
course, it never occurred to us to ask. However, soon after this
my aunt took me through a book which I still have, called The
Child's Introduction to Thoroughbass in Conversations
of a Fortnight between a Mother and her Daughter aged
Ten years old. . . .

At seven, Ralph received his earliest instruction in violin-playing
(he recalled that 'a wizened old German called Cramer appeared
on the scene and gave me my first lesson'), tackled Stainer's
Harmony, and began a correspondence course in music theory run
by the University of Edinburgh, passing both preliminary and
advanced grades under Aunt Sophy's tutelage. But as an arbiter
of musical good taste, Aunt Sophy held views that typified Victorian upper middle class conservatism and starchy cultural preju-
dice; Haydn it seemed, was 'Good', but Strauss waltzes 'Vulgar';
one can imagine the confusion caused by Ralph's discovery that
the second subject group of the opening movement of Haydn's
Symphony No.103 in E flat, the *'Drum-Roll'*, was, to all intents and
purposes, a waltz!

Meanwhile, Ralph had been presented with a toy theatre, for
which he wrote little operas (his manuscript book, headed *Overtures by Mr R.V. Williams*, includes sketches for *'The Major'*, *'The
Ram Opera'*, and the equally improbable *'Galoshes of Happiness'*),
and produced several piano miniatures, all *'respectfully dedicated to
Miss Sophy Wedgwood'*. In September 1883, Ralph followed his
brother Hervey to a preparatory school at Rottingdean. It was a
severe, regimented environment, founded upon the combined
virtues of industriousness, integrity, and character-building, its
remit zealously maintained as only a Victorian educational estab-
lishment knew how. The boys rose at six-thirty, subsisted on
bread and butter, stodge puddings, and the occasional sliver of
coarse beef, supplemented by kippers and chocolate purchased
from a local victuallers shop in the High Street. Baths, one a week
for each boy, were taken briskly before prep.

But music was a prominent part of the curriculum; Ralph
received piano instruction from Mr A.C. West, whom he remembered as a fine and cultivated musician who introduced him to
Bach's *'48'* (his *Preludes and Fugues*) in a simplified edition by

Berthold Tours, while his violin tuition was now placed in the hands of a visiting Manxman who travelled up weekly from his lodgings in Brighton – one W.M. Quirke.

'The climax of my career at Rottingdean,' explained the composer decades later, 'was when I played Raff's *Cavatina* at a school concert.' Half a century after the event, he still remembered this once-familiar salon miniature, as he demonstrated by seizing the eminent W.H. Reed's violin (a former close associate of Sir Edward Elgar, Reed had been engaged as orchestra leader at the Three Choirs Festival) and playing the piece 'double-stops and all!', to the great delight of the assembled company.

The second master at Rottingdean, Billy Hewitt, took him to hear one of the great Hans Richter's concerts in Brighton. The programme, of Beethoven, Weber, and Wagner, thrilled him; *The Ride of the Valkyries* became one of his staples for out-of-earshot extemporisation back at the school, where he preferred to call it *The Charge of the Light Brigade!* Vaughan Williams's years at Rottingdean were otherwise undistinguished (save for his uncanny facility in the declension of irregular Greek verbs), and in 1887, he joined his brother at Charterhouse, then as now one of the most progressive and enlightened among English public schools.

Carthusian music-making was supervised by a number of outstanding musicians, including the organist H.G. Robinson, a Mr Becker, who played both piano and French horn, an undermaster named Steward ('Stewfug' to the boys) who bolstered the violas of the school orchestra, and a certain Mr 'Duck' Girdlestone, choral and orchestral conductor, and enthusiastic if execrable amateur cellist. Vaughan Williams received one of his first practical lessons in orchestration when, in the slow movement of Beethoven's *Symphony No.1 in C*, he discovered that Becker's horn pedal-note enriched the repeated quavers of the viola section, in which he now found himself. Meanwhile, Sunday afternoons brought frequent invitations to participate in impromptu readthroughs of string concertos from the Italian Baroque at the home of Mr Girdlestone.

In August 1888, Ralph and his schoolfriend H.Vivian Hamilton (later a successful pianist) took the bold and unprecedented step of approaching the Headmaster, Dr. Haig Brown, requesting permission to use the school hall to present a concert of their own compositions. It was an act of cavalier temerity, for: 'Headmasters were Headmasters in those days, not the hail-fellow-well-met-young-feller-me-lads of modern times . . . ' – and the formidable Haig Brown was certainly no exception. Nonetheless, permission was granted, and the concert, which included Vaughan Williams's single-movement piano trio, went ahead.

The mathematics master, James Noon, congratulated the young composer afterwards 'in the sepulchral voice that Carthusians of my day knew so well . . . "Very good, Williams. You must go on" – I treasured this as one of the very few words of encouragement I received in my life!'

CHAPTER 2
LONDON, CAMBRIDGE, HOLST, AND ADELINE
(1890–1903)

- ◆ *Oberammergau, Agnosticism, and Wagner*
- ◆ *At the Royal College of Music – Parry*
- ◆ *The Cambridge Years*
- ◆ *London again – Stanford*
- ◆ *Vaughan Williams and Gustav Holst*
- ◆ *Marriage to Adeline Fisher*
- ◆ *Bruch and Berlin*

The summer months of 1890 marked the onset of a period of intense self-discovery for Ralph. He had left Charterhouse in July, and during the first part of the holidays, he accompanied his mother, Aunt Sophy, brother Hervey, and sister Margaret on a tour which took them first to Oberammergau, for the Passion Play. The fervently devotional atmosphere, together with the archaic ritual and oppressive dogma associated with the spectacle fostered in Vaughan Williams a keen revulsion, and brought into sharper relief a mounting awareness of just how little religious faith and practice meant to him.

Although confirmed into the Church of England while at Charterhouse, he made no secret of the fact that he attended its services only 'so as not to upset the family'. Ralph had harboured atheistic views (about which he then wisely kept his own counsel) as a schoolboy, but later at Cambridge his philosophy drifted towards openly professed agnosticism. Yet his love for the King James Authorized Version of the Bible of 1611 would remain undiminished throughout his life; he drew constant inspiration from the grandeur and beauty of its Jacobean English idiom, but his absorption in music somehow obviated any need for commonplace observance.

But after an unpromising start in Oberammergau, the vacation yielded another – and this time, truly seismic – spiritual encounter. It was in Munich that Ralph had his first experience of Wagnerian music-drama. Both the event and its revelatory aftermath were later described in the composer's autobiography:

> *We found that* Die Walküre *was down for that evening. The opera, we were told, would start at 7, so at 6 o'clock we sat down to have a preliminary meal. Hardly had we started when the waiter rushed in – he had made a mistake, on a Wagner abend the opera started at 6. The rest decided for dinner, but I, like the hero of a novel, 'left my food untasted' and rushed off to the Opera House. I arrived just in time to hear that wonderful passage for strings when Sieglinde offers Siegmund the cup. This was my first introduction to later Wagner, but I experienced no surprise, but rather that strange certainty that I had heard it all before. There was a feeling of recognition as of meeting an old friend, which comes to us all in the face of great artistic experiences. I had the same experience when I first heard an English folk-song, when I first saw Michelangelo's* Day and Night, *when I first came upon Stonehenge, or had my first sight of New York City – the intuition that I had been there already.*

Founded in 1883 by Sir George Grove, first editor of the *Grove Dictionary of Music and Musicians*, the Royal College of Music appeared from its inception to distance itself from the entrenched artistic conservatism of Victorian society. Musical life offered little respite from lugubrious oratorio performances (for orchestral concerts were rare outside the larger cities), with Mendelssohn's choral works, and the gargantuan performances of Handel's *Messiah* (often involving hundreds of performers) then much in vogue forming the backbone of music-making in these islands.

Sir George, an enlightened thinker and idealist whose interests ranged far beyond the exclusively musical, encouraged his students toward a universal perception of all the arts, underlining the importance of the cross-fertilization of concepts and ideas within various disciplines, even the practical and scientific. Thus enabled to discern the greater picture, RCM students found a means of escape from the stifling priggishness that seemed endemic in British music of the day. Vaughan Williams had long since made up his mind that he wished to study there, and with one man whose music seemed to embody his own artistic and personal aspirations.

> *I was determined if possible to study composition under Parry. I had first heard of Parry some years before, when I was still a schoolboy. I remember my cousin, Stephen Massingberd, coming into the room full of that new book* Studies of Great Com-posers. *'This man Parry,' he said, 'declares that a composer must write music as his musical conscience demands.' This was quite a new idea to me, the loyalty of an artist to his art. Soon after that I got to know some of his music, especially parts of* Judith, *and I remember, even as a boy, my brother saying to me that there was something, to his mind, peculiarly English about his music. So I was quite prepared to join with the other young students at the RCM in worship at that shrine, and I think I can truly say that I have never been disloyal to it.*

When Vaughan Williams entered the Royal College of Music in September 1890, the student body would have numbered rather less than one hundred all told. Under Grove's directorship, the teaching faculty recruited that celebrated triumvirate whose compositions buttressed Victorian music life in concert room, church, and theatre: Sir Hubert Parry, Sir Charles Villiers Stanford, and Sir Arthur Sullivan. The College maintained close links with the Universities of Oxford and Cambridge (the Chair in Music at Oxford was held by Parry from 1900–8, while Stanford's professorship at Cambridge spanned the period 1887–1924), with the music of the Church of England and, through Sullivan's operettas, with the London stage.

College protocol decreed, however, that no would-be student of composition was permitted to undertake the course without first passing the higher internal (Grade V) examination in harmony. Ralph spent his first two terms at the RCM working through Macfarren's *Harmony* under Dr. F.E. Gladstone, first cousin of the great Liberal statesman, and a renowned organist and prolific composer of church music. During the spring term of 1891, with the required examination now behind him, Vaughan Williams was permitted to join Parry's composition class. He described himself as:

> ... *very elementary at the time. I blush with shame at the horrible little songs and anthems which I presented for his criticism. Parry's great watchword was 'characteristic'.... Before telling the following story, I ought to explain that Parry, not content with the official lesson, used to keep his pupil's compositions to look at during the week. One day, through pure carelessness, I had written out a scale passage with one note repeated and then a gap (i.e., CDEFGGBC instead of CDEFGABC). Parry said: 'I have been looking at this passage for a long time to discover whether it is just a mistake, or whether you meant anything characteristic!'*

In the late 20th century, even the most modestly equipped music-lover enjoys the benefits of instant replay and studio-quality hi-fi sound. Never before in its history has music from every genre and period been so widely accessible; so much so, in fact, that it is sometimes hard to realize that things were not ever thus. As Vaughan Williams explained:

> *Before the gramophone and the wireless and the miniature score, the pianoforte duet was the only way, unless you were an orchestral player, of getting to know orchestral music, and one really got to know it from the inside; not in the superficial way of lazily listening to a gramophone record.*

Perhaps he could have been a little more forgiving of his own limited musical horizons at the time, describing himself, in his 1953 memoirs, as 'painfully illiterate in those days, even more so than now'.

> *Parry could hardly believe that I knew so little music. One day he was talking to me about the wonderful climax in the development of the* 'Appassionata' *Sonata (Beethoven's* Piano Sonata No. 23 in F Minor, *Op. 57). Suddenly he realized that I did not know it, so he sat down at the pianoforte and played it through to me. There were showers of wrong notes, but in spite of that, it*

> *was the finest performance that I have ever heard. So I was told to study Beethoven, especially the late quartets, 'as a religious exercise'.*

A man of patrician values and radical political leanings, Parry (who declared that 'the composition of the House of Lords might be improved by the admission of a few burglars!') found certain popular musical forms, notably French opera, understandably repugnant, exhorting his students to 'write choral music as befits an Englishman and a democrat'. Vaughan Williams wrote of his influence and scholarship in these terms:

> *We pupils of Parry have, if we have been wise, inherited from him the great English choral tradition which Tallis passed on to Byrd, Byrd to Gibbons, Gibbons to Purcell, Purcell to Battishill and Greene, and they in their turn through the Wesleys to Parry. He has passed on the torch to us and it is our duty to keep it alight. . . . I hereby solemnly declare, keeping steadily in view the works of Byrd, Purcell, and Elgar, that Parry's* Blest Pair of Sirens *is my favourite piece of music written by an Englishman.*

Among Ralph's student contemporaries at the time, one name stands alone – that of Richard Walthew (1872–1952) – not by reason of any great musical gifts, save a proselytising desire to share with his friends the chance to experience the widest cross-section of music. Vaughan Williams occasionally joined him at his home in Highbury to play piano duet reductions of new works ('he played and I stumbled behind him as best I could!'), including Sir Charles Villiers Stanford's *Irish Symphony*. Now convinced that Bach, Beethoven, Brahms, and Wagner were the only composers worthy of his attention, a reluctant visit with Walthew ('who had a holy terror of anything high falutin' in art') to hear Bizet's *Carmen* proved decisive:

> *I went prepared to scoff, but Walthew won the day and I remained to pray. It must have been about the same time that I had another salutary disturbance of my musical prejudices: I heard Verdi's* Requiem *for the first time. At first I was properly shocked by the frank sentimentalism and sensationalism*

of the music.' But in a very few minutes the music possessed me. I realized that here was a composer who could do all the things which I, with my youthful pedantry, thought wrong.... That day I learnt that there is nothing in itself that is 'common or unclean', indeed that there are no canons of art except that contained in the well-worn adage 'To thine own self be true.'

Sir Hubert Parry made his personal library of orchestral scores freely available to his personal students. Ralph borrowed copies of Wagner's *Siegfried* and *Tristan und Isolde*, and later remembered that, for some time after studying the *German Requiem* of Johannes Brahms, his own efforts consisted largely of variants on a passage near the start of that work. Richard Walthew asked to borrow the score of Wagner's *Parsifal* prelude, and was dismayed by Parry's censure of the piece as 'mere scene-painting'. We may only speculate as to Parry's likely response to Debussy's *Prélude à l'après-midi d'un faune* (written at much the same time, 1892), or Arnold Schoenberg's *Verklärte Nacht* (1899); both were to change the entire course of western music irrevocably. Vaughan Williams suggested that to Parry, form was always pre-eminent over colour, and that he exhibited an 'almost moral abhorrence of luscious sound'. Perhaps this went some way to explaining the negative response in some quarters to Parry's conservatism, and to his Germanically-influenced orchestration. 'The truth is, I think,' concluded Vaughan Williams, 'that he occasionally went too far in deliberate eschewal of orchestral effect. . . . I was sitting next to Elgar at a rehearsal of Parry's *Symphonic Variations* with its curious spiky sound. I said, 'I suppose many people would call this bad orchestration; I do not find it so.' Elgar turned on me almost fiercely: 'Of course it's not bad orchestration, the music could have been scored in no other way.'

On 15 June 1892, the Royal Opera House, Covent Garden, presented the first London performance of *Tristan* since Wagner himself had directed its English premiere seventeen years earlier. It was a momentous occasion; a distinguished cast including Max Alvary and Rosa Sucher in the title roles was conducted by Gustav Mahler. Later that evening, as Ralph stood waiting for a train on a dimly-lit Underground platform at Charing Cross, clutching Parry's score beneath his arm, he met a student acquaintance who had attended the performance with Cambridge undergraduate

George McCleary. This chance encounter marked the start of a long friendship, although long years would pass before Ralph finally admitted to McCleary that he had been deeply shaken by *Tristan*. The Dowager Lady Farrer, also a student in Parry's composition class, sometimes witnessed the last few minutes of Ralph's lessons, which invariably over-ran. After one exacting and mildly confrontational session, Parry seemed more than usually perplexed as Ralph gathered his sheaves of manuscript paper and left the room; 'That's a very strange young man', declared Parry. 'He says he can't sleep at all after he's heard one of Wagner's operas!'

With two years of study at the Royal College behind him, Cambridge beckoned. Ralph entered Trinity College in October 1892, and was not without family connections there. His cousin Ralph Wedgwood, already metamorphosed from freshman into popular Cantabrian socialite, ensured that his young relative was never lonely. Ralph wrote of what he termed the 'Magic Circle' of Wedgwood's friends, who included the eminent historian George Trevelyan, the lawyer P. Maurice Sheldon-Amos, and the author of *Principia Ethica*, the philosopher G.E. Moore.

Camaraderie and friendship extended beyond the Cambridge terms, and holidays were often spent at Seatoller, in Borrowdale, where politics, theology, natural philosophy, and the arts were avidly debated, and new books consumed at a rate of knots. In later years, three of the five would receive the Order of Merit, and Ralph Wedgwood a knighthood, and Chief General Managership of the London and North Eastern Railway Company. The two Ralphs were also made welcome at the houses of the Darwin family in Cambridge, but for Vaughan Williams, it would be the visits made to the Lodge at Downing College that would shape his future most dramatically. Herbert Fisher, late of Brockenhurst, Hampshire (before settling with his family in Surrey), had known Ralph's father and uncles well, and a strong friendship had developed between the two families. Florence, the eldest daughter of Herbert Fisher, an erudite beauty and a capable amateur violinist, had married Frederick Maitland, an authority on British legal history, and Cambridge law professor, and their home at Downing College hosted a constant procession of musical visitors.

Joining with the two Gatty brothers, Nicholas and Ivor

(players of violin and horn respectively), Vaughan Williams and his viola were among the most enthusiastic and frequent visitors to Downing Lodge, where 'scratch' chamber music sessions took place weekly. Sometimes Florence's younger sister Adeline joined in as cellist, although her real talent lay at the piano keyboard. Demure, graceful, articulate and gentle, Adeline (fifth of the eleven children born to the Fishers) was staying at the lodge in June 1893 when the Maitlands welcomed Tchaikovsky as a guest. Florence and Adeline both pinned roses in his buttonhole before he left to join Saint-Saëns, Bruch, and Boito, as the four composers received honorary degrees from the University.

Although officially reading history, Ralph devoted the greater part of his time and energies to music, travelling regularly to London to attend Parry's classes. He was also receiving coaching from Charles Wood in preparation for his Bachelor of Music degree. Wood had become organist at Caius College in 1891, and was destined to spend the remainder of his days in Cambridge. Unobtrusive and retiring by nature, Wood was a phenomenally gifted teacher and a superb all-round musician; 'Charles Wood was the finest technical instructor I have ever known . . . for the craft of composition he was unrivalled, and he managed to teach me enough to pull me through my B. Mus. I also had organ lessons from Alan Gray. Our friendship survived his despair at my playing, and I became quite expert at managing the stops for his voluntaries and recitals.'

Then as now, Cambridge offered a bewildering range of musical activity to its charges. Ralph had spent his freshman year in rooms at 17 Magdalene Street, and moved thereafter to No.2 Whewells Court. An enthusiastic member of the University Music Club, he sang regularly, and on Sunday mornings conducted a small choir in Schubert's masses. The Music Club arranged regular recitals of chamber music on Saturday evenings in termtime, and Vaughan Williams, who seems never to have taken part as a performer, was widely respected as both critic and adviser by those who did, including the organ scholar from Christ's College, Hugh Allen, of whom he said:

> *I believe I had the honour of first introducing him to the music of Brahms. . . . Allen at once took over the University Music Club, shook them out of their complacency, and made them rehearse*

> *such things as the Schumann and Brahms pianoforte quintets and Schubert's* String Quintet. *I got much musical instruction in listening to the rehearsal of these works, which I came to know nearly by heart.*

Saturday evenings had their serious side, but post-concert pere-grinations were often uproariously funny. With his keen sense of the ridiculous and the parodistic, Vaughan Williams would surely have taken nefarious delight in the Trinity Don Sedley Taylor's spoof on Sullivan's parlour-room ballad *The Lost Chord*, which reportedly began with 'Batting one day at the Oval . . . ' It was, moreover, at one of these gatherings that Ralph heard one of his own works performed in public for the first time. It was a quartet for men's voices:

> *The second tenor got a bar out and remained so nearly to the end. Allen organized an encore and it was done all over again, this time correctly. The audience disliked it the second time even more than the first. This may seem a small episode, but it was my first experience of an essential and salutary, though unpleas-ant, form of composition lesson. . . . Allen did me the same service, though on a larger scale, in 1910, when after my* Sea Symphony *had had a very doubtful reception at the Leeds Festival, he at once arranged for performances at Oxford and in London, though he confessed to me afterwards that he was rather frightened about it.*

At Easter, 1895, 'The Magic Circle' spent their last holiday together at Seatoller. Vaughan Williams had passed his B.Mus. examination during the previous year, but the summer months beckoned with the promise of little but hard work in prospect, as the history finals loomed ominously close.

Ralph obtained an upper-second pass; not an especially impressive achievement, but he could now return to London, and to musical study, without other distractions. Charles Wood ex-pressed little hope for him as a composer, and the organist Alan Gray, too, had written already to Sir Walter Parratt, Professor of Organ at the Royal College, whose charge his former student would shortly become, voicing grave reservations as to his capa-bilities at the organ bench:

I wish you would let me have a line as to your opinion of Vaughan Williams. He is leaving here next term and is uncertain as to his future ... he seems to me somewhat hopeless, but I should be very glad if you could give me your opinion, as of course you have far wider experience than I in such matters.

Several of Vaughan Williams's earliest published works date from his undergraduate years. Two of a set of three *Elizabethan part-songs* issued in 1896 had been written before he left the RCM for Trinity, Cambridge, but his most familiar song setting from this early period, '*Whither must I wander*', dates from 1894, the year in which he obtained his Bachelor of Music degree, although it would remain unpublished until 1912.

When Vaughan Williams enrolled as a student at the Royal College for the second time, mid-way through the midsummer term of 1895, England was reeling at the infamous revelations made public during the trial of Oscar Wilde. The after-shock of scandal reached every level of society, and nothing, it seemed, would ever be quite the same again. But in the world of music, several brilliant young stars were now in the ascendant; Claude Debussy and Frederic Delius were both thirty-three, and Edward Elgar was in his thirty-eighth year. In the concert hall, it was the dashing Henry Wood, then just twenty-six, who was bringing much unfamiliar music, often by as yet obscure composers, before the eager public who flocked to support his recently established promenade concerts. At the college, Parry had taken over as Director, and Vaughan Williams continued his formal studies in composition under Sir Charles Villiers Stanford:

Stanford was a great teacher, but I believe I was unteachable ... the details of my work annoyed Stanford so much that we seldom arrived at the broader issues and the lesson usually started with a conversation along these lines: 'Damnably ugly, my boy! why do you write such things?' 'Because I like them.' 'But you can't like them, they're not music.' 'I shouldn't write them if I didn't like them.'

So the argument went on, and there was never any time left for constructive criticism. .... Stanford never really displayed great enthusiasm for my work. I once showed him a movement of a quartet which had caused me hours of agony, and I thought it would really move mountains this time. 'All rot, my boy,' was his only comment.

Ralph became acquainted at this time with the thirty-one-year-old Gustav von Holst, whom he later described as 'the greatest influence on my music'. The pair shared identical aspirations, and each displayed a seriousness of purpose that has prompted some sources to liken their association to that of Goethe and Schiller. Holst (he later dropped the 'von') came from a family of professional musicians, and had joined the RCM on a £30 scholarship in 1895. The privations of the musician's lot did nothing to deter him, although he supplemented his income by playing the trombone in the Scottish Orchestra and for the Carl Rosa Opera Company, and would usually be away on tour during college holidays. The two students held regular 'field days', in which they played new works to each other, and sought advice and criticism. That each voiced opinions with a degree of frankness which might have caused offence in other, less musically dedicated circles, is a tribute to the depth of their friendship and mutual respect. Their 'field day' meetings would continue until Holst's death nearly forty years later, and it is quite probable that there was no major work produced by either which was not shown to the other for comment.

Ralph also joined the College debating society, and delivered papers on a wide range of subjects, including the music of Henry Purcell, the rise and fall of Romanticism, Wagner's festivals at Bayreuth, and the importance of didactic art. Holst and Vaughan Williams met regularly with other students, including John Ireland, Thomas Dunhill, Fritz Hart and others 'in a little teashop in Kensington, to discuss every subject under the sun, from the lowest note of the double bassoon to the philosophy of *Jude the Obscure*.' Vaughan Williams's recollection of these occasions in his 1953 autobiography includes this footnote:

I learnt more from these conversations than from any amount of formal teaching, but I felt at a certain disadvantage with these companions: they were all so competent, and I felt such an amateur. I have struggled all my life to conquer amateurish technique and now that perhaps I have mastered it, it seems too late to make any use of it.

Ralph had maintained his associations with the Fisher family, and in the process, had fallen deeply in love with Adeline, whom he had met frequently while at Cambridge where she had often taken the cellist's seat in a string quartet, affectionately known as the 'Cowley Street Wobblers', that had included Vaughan Williams as violist.

As Ursula Vaughan Williams writes: 'There was everything in the way of background and interest to draw them together. Ralph, deep in pre-Raphaelite poetry, saw all romance alive in her beauty, and devoted himself to writing piano music to give her pleasure.' They became engaged after Ralph left the RCM in the summer of 1896, and were married at St Barnabas' Church, South Lambeth, on 9 October 1897. Ralph had taken the post of organist there two years earlier, and loathed every minute of it, writing in despair to Holst about the 'louts' of the choir, 'who slope into choir practice half an hour after it has begun'.

Ralph had decided to extend a planned honeymoon in Germany with a period of study in Berlin. Armed with a letter of introduction to Heinrich von Herzogenberg, head of composition at the Hochschule für Musik in Berlin (from the pen of a reluctant Stanford, who urged him to visit Italy instead), and spurred on by the knowledge that the Berlin State Opera was about to stage the whole of Wagner's *Ring* without cuts, the young composer, seduced at the time by the might of German Romanticism, saw Berlin as the place to be. Herzogenberg proposed a course of lessons with Max Bruch, a composer with British connections in Liverpool (he had written the celebrated *Violin Concerto in G minor*, and the *Scottish Fantasia*, and was director of the Liverpool Philharmonic Society from 1881 until 1883), and his music had made a strong impression on Vaughan Williams, who had heard much of it performed in England. Ralph wrote with obvious gratitude of the support and encouragement he received from Bruch, and relished the wealth of concerts and opera performances that Berlin offered.

I heard all the music I could, especially operas. Among them were Lortzing's Undine *and Meyerbeer's* Robert le Diable. *I also remember beautiful performances of Bach cantatas at the Singakademie. The Joachim and Halir Quartets were at their zenith and there was a memorable performance at the Hochschule of the*

Brahms Double Concerto *played as a pianoforte trio by Joachim, Hausman and Barth.*

Christmas 1897 was spent with Adeline's parents in San Remo, and Ralph, like Berlioz and Liszt before him, found Italy a place of inspiration and opportunity. After the dank greyness of Berlin, the brilliant sunshine of crisp winter days in more southerly climes permitted long walks and even cycle excursions. In early January 1898, the couple returned to Berlin for Ralph's final study sessions with Bruch, which continued on a weekly basis for the next three months. The great conductor Arthur Nikisch directed the last of the season's Philharmonic concerts at the beginning of April, and one week later Ralph and Adeline were back at Leith Hill Place. Officially, Ralph was still organist at St Barnabas' Church, South Lambeth, and the couple found rooms at 16 North Street, Westminster, before settling at 5 Cowley Street. In fact, they had been turned out of North Street because, as Adeline explained when writing to her mother with details of their new address 'the landlady had objected strongly to me having influenza!'

Her letter continues 'My husband has not done any composition since he set foot in England – nor has he wished to – he works tremendously hard at his choir and organ and piano . . . ' The facts as Adeline described them were accurate, but in reality, Vaughan Williams still doubted his readiness to embark upon the *via crucis* of the professional composer. In 1900, he wrote to Elgar, seeking his help and guidance in orchestration, and received a polite rebuttal from Lady Elgar, and the suggestion that Granville Bantock might be a suitable teacher. Ralph later wrote that 'though Elgar would not teach me personally, he could not help teaching me through his music. I spent several hours at the British Museum studying the full scores of the *'Enigma' Variations* and *The Dream of Gerontius*. The results are obvious in the opening pages of the Finale of my *Sea Symphony*. . . . '

In 1901, Vaughan Williams completed his Doctorate in Music at Cambridge, but even this decisive academic milestone did not signal the end of his musical education, for he had yet to savour what he liked to call 'a little French polish' from Maurice Ravel. Having resigned his organist's post, he devoted his energies to composing numerous songs, only to withold most from publication – in some cases for many years – while destroying others with which he was dissatisfied.

Many of Vaughan Williams's most celebrated vocal settings date from the early 1900s; the popular '*Linden Lea*', to lines by the Dorset dialect poet William Barnes, was composed in 1900 yet not issued until 1912. In addition to settings of Pre-Raphaelite texts by the Rossettis (*The House of Life*, six settings of poems by Dante Gabriel Rossetti date from 1903), Tennyson, Herbert and Shakespeare provided sources of inspiration, as did Robert Louis Stevenson. '*Whither must I Wander?*', finally issued as the seventh of Vaughan Williams's famous cycle of Stevenson settings, *Songs of Travel* (1907), was in fact written around the turn of the century, and first circulated in a 1902 issue of the journal *The Vocalist*.

The immediate future seemed secure, although Ralph contined to give University Extension lectures, and contributed articles on 'Fugue' and 'Conducting' to the forthcoming 1904 edition of Grove's Dictionary. He also edited two volumes of songs for the Purcell Society, and agonized privately over his concern that the personal, characteristic musical voice he sought eluded him, describing himself as 'stale, dried up, and prematurely decayed' in his letters to Gustav Holst. But in May 1902, he issued what amounted to his own creative manifesto, in a letter published in *The Vocalist* :

> *What we want in England is* real *music, even if it be only a music-hall song. Provided it possesses real feeling and real life, it will be worth all the off-scourings of the classics in the world.*

CHAPTER 3

FOLK-SONGS, HYMNS, AND PARIS . . .
(1903–8)

- *Interest in English Folk-song*
- *Contributions to Grove's Dictionary*
- *The English Hymnal*
- *'A little French polish' – studies with Ravel*

O ne summer's afternoon in 1903, a workman eased his toil in song as he tended the verdant lawns and bee-favoured floral borders of an English country house. Visiting that house in Hambridge, Somerset, at the time, was one Cecil J. Sharp (1859–1924), a scholar and teacher who would be the first in these islands to recognize the beauty and significance of traditional song and devote his life's work to its preservation and understanding. Sharp and Vaughan Williams had met three years earlier, but although Bartók and Kodály were already collecting folk-songs in the by-ways and villages of Hungary, there was as yet no comparable movement in England. The English Folksong Society had been founded in 1898 with precisely these objectives in view, yet it had amassed fewer than one hundred songs by the time Vaughan Williams became a member in 1904. In a vehement letter intended to expose the complacency of the society, Cecil Sharp asserted that its members should leave the plush London clubs in which they met, and venture into the fields and villages of rural England, to hear at first hand the songs of country folk.

The idea was not a new one; the followers of William Morris recognized that his art was rooted in the spirit of decorative styles that had been practised by village craftsmen for centuries. Such ideas appealed powerfully to Gustav Holst, who had joined the Morris circle in an effort to develop his own creative originality, hoping to avoid any 'off-scouring the classics' in his music.

Long before Vaughan Williams commenced serious field work on rural England's vocal heritage, he had become familiar with several early volumes of folk-songs, principally John Broadwood's 1889 collection with harmonies by H.F. Birch Reynardson, *Sussex Songs*. In 1893, J.A. Fuller Maitland issued the first detailed study of indigenous English folk-song, *English Country Songs*, a work which Ralph regarded as a major contribution to English musical and social history. It seemed natural that one of his 1902 University Extension lectures should examine *The Characteristics of National Songs in the British Isles*, and his comments, first heard in a crowded assembly hall at the Technical School, Pokesdown, Bournemouth, were widely reported in the musical press.

At the end of March, Sir Dan Godfrey conducted the Bournemouth Municipal Orchestra at the town's Winter Gardens in Vaughan Williams's *Bucolic Suite*, in a programme that also included Holst's *Cotswold Symphony*. Both works were favourably received, but Ralph's thoughts were elsewhere. He would soon repeat his lectures in Gloucester and, later, in Brentwood, Essex.

After one occasion, he was invited to a tea-party arranged by the Reverend Heatley, Vicar of Ingrave, for the elderly residents of the Parish, some of whom might well know some local songs. Overcoming both his shyness and a certain scepticism, Ralph accepted the invitation. The vicar's daughters presented a venerable elder to him, announcing him as 'Mr. Pottipher'. Although he would not sing in front of his neighbours at tea, Mr. Pottipher explained that he would happily sing the next day, if Ralph would call at his house. On 4 December 1903, Vaughan Williams noted down the song '*Bushes and Briars*' and later recalled that:

> . . . *here, as before with Wagner, I had that same sense of recognition – "here's something which I have known all my life – only I didn't know it!" . . . this same sense had come on me in 1893, when I discovered* 'Dives and Lazarus' *in* English Country Songs.

Back at Leith Hill Place for the Christmas holiday, he continued to track down more songs, this time on his own doorstep, during bicycling jaunts made with pencil and notebook at the ready. In early January he visited Mr. Pottipher again, and took down more songs from him. In the village of Barton Street, he heard local gypsies singing ballads, and managed to obtain copies of their entire repertoire, including the song '*William and Phillis*'. During March, he cycled for ten days around Essex, visiting Willingale, Ingrave, Little Burstead, East Horndon, and Billericay, noting down more material as he went. During this one period alone, Vaughan Williams took down '*Green Bushes*', '*John Barleycorn*', '*The Farmer's Boy*', and four local variants of '*The Lost Lady Found*'. In April, his bicycle took him into Norfolk, where he obtained traditional folk-songs in the area around King's Lynn. A holiday in Yorkshire during the summer of 1904 brought fresh avenues for exploration, and he located several new titles in Westerdale and at Robin Hood's Bay, and finished a remarkably fruitful period of research in the Wiltshire villages of Stratford Tony, Ramsbury, and Coombe Bissett, near Salisbury, at the end of August.

Given that, on his own admission, Vaughan Williams was still searching for his own identity as a composer, it is not altogether surprising that some commentators have described his mature style as an anachronism – a less-than-fully-developed personal idiom spiced and fertilized by folk melody. But in reality, his deep involvement with folk-song proved to be the catalyst that released his own characteristic idiom. Leaving aside regional and ethnic concerns, how did his experiences in the field shape his creative evolution as a composer? – after all, were not Bartók and Kodály following a broadly similar course? To find the answer to these questions, one must consider the debate that followed in the English press in October 1904, over the vexed question of what constituted genuine folk-song. Ironically enough, Vaughan Williams's research revealed a major flaw in the 'official' view put forward by the English Folksong Society. Stanford, for example, held that most English folk-songs could not, and never had shared the interval of a flattened seventh, which Vaughan Williams had always thought characteristic of the genre. Stanford's views represented those preached by the society, none of whose members had actually bothered to go out into the countryside to test the hypothesis!

A series of exchanges in *The Morning Post* fuelled discussion on this and other questions, and crystallized in Vaughan Williams a growing self-assurance and authority which, in turn, liberated a strongly independent and original musical personality, powerfully revealed in several compositions that emerged over the next few years. But the experience of collecting folk-songs by mingling with country folk who had handed them from generation to generation forged a new alliance between Vaughan Williams and Cecil Sharp, who helped to prepare over sixty folk-songs for publication in the *Journal of English Folksong*, Volume I.

And yet how could a serious, purposeful young composer, steeped as much in the Teutonic grandeur of the post-Lisztian epoch as in the heritage of the great English polyphonists of whom he was a natural heir, give voice to folk-song in his own works? Ever since Liszt penned his first *Hungarian Rhapsody* in 1846, the quasi-improvisatory, often gaudily virtuosic 'Rhapsody' had ended the search for a creative conduit through which to express nationalist sentiment in music. In its simplest form, the medium presented a seamless tapestry of unrelated material, normally of folkloristic origin, as a continuous whole.

By the beginning of this century, and into its first few decades, almost every musical nation had expressed something of itself in this way. In Sweden, Hugo Alfvén's three *Swedish Rhapsodies* became hugely popular; in the folklore of his native Romania, George Enescu found the impulse for his own *Romanian Rhapsodies*, and Bartók's *Dance Suite* of 1923 turned out to be a rhapsody in all but name, whereas Janáček's Gogol-inspired masterpiece *Taras Bulba* (1915–18) is the quintessential orchestral rhapsody to end them all.

Between 1905 and 1907, Vaughan Williams composed his three *Norfolk Rhapsodies*, which contain many of the characteristic folk melodies collected among the fisherfolk of King's Lynn. Only the first of the trilogy has found favour in the concert hall, and for good reason; its main themes are the beautiful folk-song melody '*The Captain's Apprentice*', and the sea shanty '*The Bold Young Sailor*'. The reflective epilogue was added when the work was extensively revised almost twenty years later. Another composition was taking shape at much the same time as the three rhapsodies. In his touchingly evocative orchestral portrait *In the Fen Country*, Vaughan Williams did not, as is often suggested, quote from regional material. In fact, he completed the score ten months before collecting his first East Anglian folk-song, although its regional idiom is unmistakable. Early sketches for *In the Fen Country* were made in 1904, in Vaughan Williams's rented office in Barton Street, Westminster. It was pure chance that his growing interest in folk-song should also coincide with his first unplanned forays into British liturgical music. One day, a visitor was ushered into his Barton Street rooms, and introduced as 'Mr. Dearmer'. The formalities were hardly over before Mr. Dearmer (Percy Dearmer: 1867–1936, an Anglican cleric, art expert, and sociologist) requested that the composer should edit a hymn-book, saying that in his opinion it should take no more than two months. Protest, it seemed, was useless! Vaughan Williams pointed out that he knew nothing whatever about hymnals, although his resistance weakened as Dearmer explained that Cecil Sharp and Canon Scott Holland had recommended him for the task. The arrangement was finally sealed when Dearmer issued a *fait accompli* that amounted to ecclesiastical blackmail. Should Vaughan Williams still refuse him, Dearmer would offer the job to a rival composer of Ralph's acquaintance!

Hymns Ancient and Modern had not found universal approval among the High Churchmen who had commisioned the 1904 revised edition, and a committee had been formed to compile a supplement. But in the event, so many texts had been assembled that music had to be found for virtually all of them, and the task of selecting the best English hymn tunes to suit the verses fell to Vaughan Williams. Dearmer's 'two-month undertaking' finally involved some two years of labour, and a personal expenditure of over £250; Dearmer had mentioned a trifling outlay of around £5. But Vaughan Williams produced the finest of all hymnals; after all, as he later remarked, 'why should we not enter into our inheritance in the church as well as the concert room?' The *English Hymnal* contains some of the finest liturgical music of these islands, as for instance in John Bunyan's great paean of faith '*He who would valiant be 'gainst all disaster . . .* ', set by Vaughan Williams to a tune named after the place at which he had first heard it – 'Monk's Gate', near Horsham, Sussex.

By his thirty-sixth year, Ralph Vaughan Williams had already played an honourable part in the British musical renaissance. October 1907 brought spectacular success with the premiere of his setting for chorus and orchestra of Walt Whitman's *Toward the Unknown Region*, in Leeds. But Ralph still felt that his technique needed further refinement. In 1908, he journeyed to Paris, settling in a single room (which lacked even a piano) in the Hôtel de l'univers et du Portugal. It would be his home for over three months. He had come to seek advice in the form of 'a little French polish' from Maurice Ravel, who, although three years his junior, had already secured international fame as a composer of greatness.

Ravel was slight, immaculate, and cultivated, and Vaughan Williams gangling, massive, and not a little self-conscious, so it is interesting to speculate upon their first meeting. Ravel suggested that his new charge should begin by composing *un petit menuet dans le style de Mozart*; it was certainly not the advice Ralph had hoped to receive, and he made his feelings plain on the matter. But during the coming weeks, the two met four or five times each week, and Ralph worked assiduously at the tasks set by Ravel, who introduced his student to piano works by Russian composers, using them as orchestration excercises.

In some respects, the influence of Maurice Ravel does indeed make itself felt in the comparative economy and new harmonic daring present in several works composed by Vaughan Williams in the aftermath of this period of study, in particular, his *G minor String Quartet*.

But it would be difficult to apply Ravel's personal musical dictum '*complexe, mais pas compliqué* ' to any other composer, which invites the question: just what did Vaughan Williams learn from him in substantive terms? The answer is enigmatic and incomplete, save for this – Ralph left Paris secure in the conviction that he was emphatically not devoid of inspiration, nor talentless, nor written out as a composer, as he had confided to Holst on more than one occasion. Ravel's confidence in his charge was, it seemed, about to be vindicated.

CHAPTER 4
FIRST TRIUMPHS
(1909–14)

- ♦ French fever
- ♦ On Wenlock Edge
- ♦ Tallis restored
- ♦ Behold the Sea . . .
- ♦ An apparition in Worcester
- ♦ A symphony for the Metropolis

As Vaughan Williams recalled, writing in an essay published in 1953:

> I came home with a bad attack of French fever and wrote a string quartet which caused a friend to say that I must have been having tea with Debussy, and a song cycle with several atmospheric effects . . .

The former, Vaughan Williams's *String Quartet in G minor*, was first heard on 8 November 1909, when it was played by the Schwiller Quartet at a meeting of the Society of British Composers. In some ways, it anticipated the multi-hued expressivity of the great *Tallis Fantasia*, but the quartet received mixed reviews, and by 1920 the critics Edwin Evans and Fox Strangways had pronounced it lost. In fact, the composer had put it aside with every intention of reviving it later, but even the second version (published in 1923) fell some way short of fully integrating its several influences.

Many listeners found the slow movement ('Romance') difficult to comprehend, the critic of the *Musical Times* describing it as 'an extreme development of modernism'. The deliciously inventive second movement ('Minuet and Trio'), with its flattened intervals and folkish idiom, bespoke an emerging personal style, although the boisterous finale ('Rondo Capriccioso') added to general consternation with multilingual performance directions (like '*sur la touche*', an instruction to string players to play over the end of the fingerboard, to produce a soft-grained, ethereal sound – a technique much favoured by Ravel) and the use of the word 'solo' in the score, indicating when prominence should be given to individual instruments. But despite adverse early press comments (*The Times* noted 'harmonic progressions that often torture the ear'), Vaughan Williams's *Quartet* is a work as charming as it seemed originally prodigal.

The song cycle *On Wenlock Edge* culls just six poems from the sixty-three that comprise A.E. Housman's anthology *A Shropshire Lad*, and employs the unusual combination of tenor voice, piano, and string quartet. The last of the set – *Clun* – might well have been started prior to Ralph's Parisian sojourn, possibly as early as 1906, and the evocative '*Is my team ploughing?* ' was included in a recital given by the tenor Gervase Elwes long before the idea of adding string parts had been envisaged. *On Wenlock Edge* was premiered in November 1909 at London's Aeolian Hall; Elwes was joined by pianist Frederick Kiddle and the members of the Schwiller Quartet. Housman's characteristic strain of fatalistic irony appealed strongly to several English composers, notably Ivor Gurney and George Butterworth, but in *On Wenlock Edge*, Vaughan Williams evinced the pallid, tragic undertones of (for example) '*Is my team ploughing?*', with its ominous dialogue between the living and the dead, with chilling realism.

The year 1909 also brought with it the incidental music (subsequently condensed into a five-movement orchestral suite) for a Cambridge production of Aristophanes' comedy *The Wasps*. The complete score, for tenor and baritone soloists, male chorus, and orchestra, was written swiftly, despite Adeline's frequent bouts of ill health. Nothing in this tumultuous *jeu d'esprit* suggests that Ralph, an able Greek scholar, found the task a less than happy diversion. The popular orchestral suite, with its brilliant overture and risible *March-Past of the Kitchen Utensils* was first presented before King George V and Queen Mary at a concert of the New Symphony Orchestra, the composer conducting, in July 1912. Although its uproarious subject matter tempts its dismissal as just good-humoured juvenilia, *The Wasps* deserves careful attention, for it reveals not just the influence of Ravel's instruction (he later described Vaughan Williams as 'the only one of my pupils who does not write my music'), but contains resonances of several Russian works that Ralph had come to know in Paris. The overture offers several glimpses, although not explicit ones, of Borodin's *Symphony No.2 in B minor*.

Michael Kennedy, author of a definitive study of Vaughan Williams's complete works, has suggested that 'Few who heard *The Wasps* music in 1909 could have imagined that the same mind was at work on the *Fantasia on a Theme by Thomas Tallis*.' In what is arguably the finest retrospective tribute ever paid to Tallis, the great Elizabethan polyphonist, Vaughan Williams gave the world an enduring masterpiece for string orchestra, in its own way quite as important as Tchaikovsky's *Serenade*, Richard Strauss's *Metamorphosen for 23 Solo Strings*, or even Arnold Schoenberg's *Verklärte Nacht*. With its distillation of fragments of the Tallis theme (the tune appears as No.92 in the *English Hymnal*), avoidance of fugal techniques, and with its constant use of the interval of the flattened seventh, the work reveals affinities between high Tudor polyphony and the world of English folk-song. This magnificent paean in the ancient modal style for double string orchestra and interpolated solo string quartet (its influence on later generations of British composers, notably Sir Michael Tippett, has been vast), was first experienced by those who attended the Gloucester Cathedral premiere in September 1910. Among them was composer Herbert Howells, who recalled the occasion nearly fifty years later, in a *Sunday Times* obituary notice for his colleague: 'Two thousand people were in the Cathedral that night, primarily to hear *Gerontius*. But there at the rostrum towered an unfamiliar, magnificent figure (thirty-nine, magisterial, dark-haired, clear cut of feature). He and a strangely new work stood between them and their devotion to Elgar. . . . '

Of all the implacable forces at large in the natural world, the sea, with its elemental ferocity, panoramic vistas and awesome serenity has catalysed more than its fair share of musical masterworks. Debussy's *La Mer*, passages of Rimsky-Korsakov's *Scheherazade*, Benjamin Britten's *Three Sea Interludes* from his opera *Peter Grimes*, and Elgar's *Sea Pictures* confirm the appeal of the maritime musical genre, before we even come to Mendelssohn's overtures *The Hebrides* and the Goethe-inspired *Calm Sea and Prosperous Voyage*. With *A Sea Symphony*, Ralph Vaughan Williams produced his first truly ground-breaking large-scale composition, not that the subject matter was unexplored by other British composers of his generation. Stanford himself had written his *Sea Songs*, and both John Ireland and Frank Bridge used the title *The Sea* in their works; then there is the superb tone-poem *Tintagel* by Arnold Bax, and the beautiful *Sea Drift* by Delius. But in his epic *Sea Symphony*, Vaughan Williams expressed those stirring emotions described by Freud (albeit in the context of religious faith) as 'that vast oceanic feeling'. When applied to *A Sea Symphony*, Freud's metaphor seems overwhelmingly potent.

This, the first of Vaughan Williams's nine symphonies, took shape over a number of years, firstly as a score headed *Songs of the Sea*, followed by a more assured 1906 reworking of many of its original ideas as an 'Oceanic Symphony', before assuming its final shape in 1909. This vast epic is scored for lavish forces; soprano and baritone soloists, mixed chorus and orchestra, with an optional organ part. The words are taken from two anthologies by Walt Whitman, *Sea Drift* (movements I–III) and *Passage to India* (movement IV); the opening section co-opts texts from two of the *Sea Drift* collection, '*Song of the Exposition*' (first published in 1871), and '*Song for All Seas, All Ships*' (1876). The second movement is a setting of *On the beach at night, alone*, published by Whitman in 1856 under the alternative title '*Clef Poem*'. Typically, this symphony views the sea in a challenging, sometimes confrontational perspective, reflecting man's ceaseless endeavours to conquer it. Only the third movement, *Scherzo* (lines from Whitman's *After the Sea-Ship*), is conventionally descriptive. The finale, headed '*The Explorers*' (lines from *Passage to India*) conveys optimistic sentiments shared by all of humanity, for the courage of endeavour is a universal thing, and the sea itself is emblematic of the brotherhood of mankind:

> *Reckless O soul, exploring I with thee, and thou with me,*
> *For we are bound where mariner has not yet dared to go,*
> *And we will risk the ship, ourselves and all.*

The premiere at Leeds Town Hall on 12 October 1910, conducted by the composer, was an astounding success; Ralph certainly never celebrated his birthday under more testing or triumphant circumstances. Preliminary rehearsals had taken place at the Royal College of Music, and many friends and family members journeyed north for the Leeds Festival performance. Vaughan Williams had been unable to eat or sleep for days previously, and when the great moment finally arrived, with the majestic brass fanfare and monumental choral invocation of the opening bars, his fears could at last be laid to rest; 'I was nearly blown off the rostrum when the chorus came in, *fortissimo – Behold the Sea itself.*'

At the end, Lady Stanford turned to Adeline with the words: 'You must be very proud of him.' Her husband, however, was more circumspect, writing in his journal that the symphony was 'Big stuff – with some impertinences.' From a generic viewpoint, *A Sea Symphony* is a curious hybrid of symphony and cantata, a condition noted at the time by the critic Hubert Foss; '*A Sea Symphony* begins and ends as a song, and as a song it is huge. As a symphony it shrinks in dimensions, belittled by its musical and technical immaturities.' Cecil Gray wrote of the symphony and its composer in these terms: 'He flounders about in the sea of his ideas like a vast and ungainly porpoise, with great puffing and blowing; yet in the end, after tremendous efforts and an almost heroic tenacity, there emerges a real and lovable personality, unassuming, modest, and almost apologetic.'

But why should music, any music, be 'original'? It was an issue that Vaughan Williams discussed in his autobiography, where he suggests that 'the object of art is to stretch out to the ultimate realities through the medium of beauty. The duty of the composer is to find the *mot juste*. It does not matter if this word has been said a thousand times before so long as it is the right thing to say at that moment.' He continues with the following interesting admission: 'I have never had any conscience about cribbing . . . the last two bars of the Scherzo to my *Sea Symphony* come from the *Mass in D*. . . . I expect Beethoven knew what he was doing when he was cribbing the last movement of the '*Appassionata*' Sonata from one of Cramer's pianoforte studies.' In the same connection, Vaughan Williams made the following, equally pertinent *apologia*: 'I am astonished to find, on looking back on my earlier works how much I cribbed from him [Elgar], probably when I thought I was being most original . . . real cribbing takes place when one composer thinks with the mind of another, even when there is no mechanical similarity of phrase.'

As Parry's diary note makes plain, Vaughan Williams's *Sea Symphony* was not above 'impertinences', nor without its idiomatic and stylistic shortcomings, but 'Big stuff' always excites, and the overwhelming visionary force of the work never lets it down in the concert hall. The very fact that *A Sea Symphony* occupies a place of renown within the English choral tradition is proof, surely, of its strengths.

The grave magnificence of the *Tallis Fantasia* paved the way for a further commission from the Worcester Festival committee, resulting in the *Five Mystical Songs* performed for the first time in September 1911, at Worcester Cathedral. Vaughan Williams chose texts by George Herbert, a poet who regarded music as 'not a science only, but a divine voice'. As Ralph's journal recollects, the premiere itself was anything but a transcendent metaphysical experience for him, though the work was rapturously received, and the occasion was one of sublime, unearthly beauty. Clare Mackail, a member of the audience and family friend, left a touching cameo of Adeline and the composer:

> *. . . with the sun shining through the windows, her hair looked like pure gold. It was an unforgettable sight, the two of them. He had a thick thatch of dark hair, a tall, rather heavy figure, even then slightly bowed; and his face was profoundly moving, deep humanity and yet with the quality of a medieval sculpture.*

For Vaughan Williams, the event was a terrifying ordeal. He had to conduct an elusive and difficult new work, unfamiliar to the orchestra and chorus. Looking over at the first violins to his left, he observed an apparition. 'I thought I was going mad, for I saw what appeared to be Kreisler (the great violin virtuoso) at a back desk. I got through somehow, and at the end I whispered to Reed (W.H. Reed, leader of the London Symphony Orchestra, and a close friend of both Elgar and Vaughan Williams), '*Am* I mad, or *did* I see Kreisler in the band?' 'Oh yes,' he said, 'he broke a string and wanted to play it in before the Elgar *Concerto* (Elgar's *Violin Concerto in B minor*) and couldn't without being heard in the Cathedral.' Ralph was an eager raconteur, and this became one of his favourite stories in later life.

Public response to revivalist compositions like *Tallis* fuelled endless academic debate on the re-awakening of interest in

England's musical heritage, most writers concluding that after centuries of slumber, our national muse was awake and rejuvenated. That Vaughan Williams selected the title 'Fantasia' (its semantic priorities are quintessentially Elizabethan) for a number of works dating from this period was no mere coincidence; in 1912 he finished scores which, though outwardly unrelated, share the same nomenclature. The *Fantasia on Christmas Carols*, for baritone soloist, chorus and orchestra, is an ingenious concoction of seasonal tunes, some less familiar today than in earlier years perhaps. Writing in *The Times* a correspondent bemoaned the fact that the work seemed to imply that 'a composer who has so much to say that is interesting should refrain from saying it, and should devote his efforts to the arrangement of other people's tunes, no matter how delightful these should be.' Frank Howes, who succeeded the carping H.C. Colles at *The Times*, and published his own study of Vaughan Williams's music in 1954 called the eight-minute *Fantasia* 'this most happy and beautiful, hearty and mystical Christmas music.'

In the realm of chamber music, Vaughan Williams returned to the Mozartian genre of the string quintet, scored for pairs of violins and violas and a single cello, dedicating his *Phantasy Quintet* to Walter Willson Cobbett and the members of the London String Quartet. Cobbett (1847–1937), a wealthy businessman, was prominent in musical circles (leading a string quartet which he financed privately), and commissioned a series of chamber works for various instruments, specifying the Elizabethan 'Fancy' or 'Fantasy' as the model. Cobbett had also instituted an important composition award in 1905, without which a wealth of new works from figures as diverse as Frank Bridge, York Bowen, Herbert Howells, Ivor Gurney, John Ireland, James Friskin, and others would never have been written. Vaughan Williams's *Phantasy Quintet*, praised by the reviewer Fox Strangways in *Music and Letters* as 'clear to the understanding and restful to the ear', secured first prize in the Cobbett Composition in 1913.

For Vaughan Williams, the creative climax of the pre-war years came with the completion, in the last weeks of 1913, of his great symphonic cameo of Edwardian London, *A London Symphony*. Much of the descriptive sentiment and fervent patriotism of Elgar's overture *Cockaigne (In London Town)*, written in the first year of this century, would be mirrored thirty-six years later in another splendid metropolitan work (alas not as popular as it deserves to be) – *A London Overture*, by John Ireland. But in *A London Symphony*, Vaughan Williams gave passionate expression to the nationalist credo he espoused in *Who wants the English Composer?* (from *National Music and Other Essays*), affirming that the composer 'should take the forms of musical expression about him and purify and raise them to the level of great art.' He continued: 'We must cultivate a sense of musical citizenship,' later proclaiming that 'It is not enough for music to come from the people, it must be for the people. . . . The ordinary man expects from a serious composer serious music and will not be frightened even at a little uplift.' The clearest statement of intent for the new symphony was enshrined in the following question: 'The lilt of the chorus at a music-hall joining in a popular song, the children dancing to a barrel-organ, the rousing fervour of a Salvation Army hymn, the cries of the street peddlers. Have not these all something to say to us?'

The germinal 'programme' for the symphony had been suggested by George Butterworth (another prodigiously gifted composer who would lose his life in the trenches of the Somme) in 1911, when Vaughan Williams had already begun sketches for a large-scale tone-poem loosely based on the life of the capital, which was to be a British counterpart to Delius's *Paris – Song of a Great City*, of 1899. Urban pictorialism in music has never lost its appeal for composers (Aaron Copland's *Quiet City* is another exercise in the genre), and after dismissing the proposal with undue haste, Vaughan Williams relented when the tremendous scope offered by a four-movement symphony crystallized into more tangible relief. He was able to play through the first two movements of the new work to his friend Cecil Armstrong Gibbs during a visit to Cambridge later that year.

A London Symphony was premiered at London's Queen's Hall on 27 March 1914, at an F.B. Ellis Concert of New Music, under the direction of Geoffrey Toye. The opening, depicting a mysterious dawn over the Thames, was inspired as much by the views from the composer's riverside home in Cheyne Walk as by the Impressionist canvasses of Claude Monet. Destined to end just as it began, this symphony's life-blood is the same great river that to H.G. Wells had been the emblem of national identity in his novel *Tono-Bungay*.

But there had been other, more subconscious influences at work, too, in the opening portrayal of the city at daybreak, when 'all that mighty heart is lying still'. The vaporous, misty introduction is built around a simple figure of four notes based on the ascending interval of a fourth. Unwittingly, Vaughan Williams had 'cribbed' this motif from the first of Debussy's *Three Symphonic Sketches – La Mer*. In 1934 he recalled that he had been 'quite unconscious that I had cribbed from *La Mer* in the introduction, until Constant Lambert horrified me by drawing my attention to it.' The triumphant first performance was greeted enthusiastically by the critics, but Vaughan Williams was dissatisfied, and subjected the score to extensive revision prior to the publication of two later versions in 1920 and 1936. As the critic H.C. Colles observed with the satirical candour for which he was noted, *A London Symphony* 'is like London itself, in that the builders will never let it alone!'

When the work was heard again in 1920 in its first revision, the conductor Albert Coates wrote his own programme note, which, despite its occasionally fanciful subjectivism, still serves the listener well in charting its course. He observed in the first movement 'daybreak by the river. Old Father Thames . . . deep and thoughtful, shrouded in mystery. Big Ben solemnly strikes the half-hour. Suddenly one is in the Strand, in the midst of the bustle and turmoil of morning traffic. . . . Then one turns off the Strand into the quiet little streets known as the Adelphi, haunted principally by beggars and ragged street-urchins. We return to the Strand and are once again caught up in the bustle and life of London.'

George Butterworth, writing in the Easter 1914 issue of the *Magazine* made some equally perceptive observations about the *Lento* slow movement: 'it is an idyll of grey skies and secluded byways – an aspect of London quite as familiar as any other. The music is remote and mystical . . . its very characteristic beauty is not of a kind which it is possible to describe in words.' Albert Coates did not agree, and set the movement in Bloomsbury. 'Dusk is falling. It is the damp and foggy twilight of a late November day. In front of a pub an old musician plays the fiddle. From the distance is heard the street-cry *Sweet Lavender, who'll buy Sweet Lavender?*' This melody, given to the solo viola, was noted by the composer in Chelsea on 21 July 1911, but topographical accuracy adds little to the impressions already noted in Butterworth's critique.

Coates felt the third movement (*Scherzo* [*Nocturne*]) sugges-tive of 'all the noises of Saturday night in the very poor quarters on the south side of the Thames, when these slums resemble a street fair, heard while one sits across the River on the Temple Embankment.'

Many commentators state the view that this was Vaughan Williams's finest orchestral essay written before the Great War. Its technical accomplishment is unmistakeable; listen out, for exam-ple, for the harp solo at the end of the movement, which reminded Frank Howes of the 'nocturnal striking of a distant Church clock'. The Finale was subjected to extensive reworking, although in its final form, its pictorialism is even more palpable. It paints the dismal tread of 'a Hunger March – ghostly marching past of those who are cold and hungry and unable to get work. . . . ' The *Symphony* ends as it began, with the river – Old Father Thames flowing calm and silent, as he has flowed through the ages, the keeper of many secrets, shrouded in mystery.'

In listening to *A London Symphony* today, we should take careful note of the composer's own comments that 'the title might run *Symphony by a Londoner*; that is to say, various sights and sounds might have influenced the composer, but it would be unhelpful to describe these. The work must succeed or fail as music, and in no other way. Therefore, if the hearers recognize a few suggestions of such things as the Westminster chimes, or the lavender cry, these must be treated as accidents and not essentials of the music.' Whether the work is viewed as descriptive, pro-grammatic, or even as its creator suggested, in purely abstract terms, matters not at all.

Gustav Holst came close to the real truth in his remark after the first performance:

> *You really have done it this time. Not only have you reached your heights, but you have taken your audience with you.*

CHAPTER 5

THE GREAT WAR AND AFTER
(1914–19)

♦ *The accidental quisling*
♦ *Not quite Officer material!*
♦ *The horrors of war*
♦ *'I sometimes dread coming back . . . '*
♦ *Service in Greece*
♦ *The teacher*

War was declared on 4 August 1914. The next day, as Ralph and Adeline (now increasingly crippled by the arthritic condition that would finally claim her) left London to spend a short vacation in Margate, thoughts of valour and patriotism, and above all, memories of those who had perished in the last great conflict, the Boer War, came implacably to the fore. Ralph sought private solace, his heart heavy with grim forebodings of catastrophe, in long walks along the cliffs overlooking the English Channel, sensing that many of those men who even now sat huddled together in the boats of the advance landing parties of the British Expeditionary Force would never return. Deep in thought, he sketched new themes in his pocket-book, until he became aware of a small boy in Scout attire, who solemnly informed him that he was now under arrest. The eager youngster marched Vaughan Williams off to the local constabulary, thinking that he had apprehended a quisling in the act of preparing maps to assist the enemy! At the police station, the suspicious manuscript paper was examined, and the dismayed composer was let off with a caution.

Talk of mobilization and imminent invasion created a ferment of activity; Britain's young men responded unhesitatingly to the call to arms, and upon returning to Cheyne Walk, Ralph learned that many of his closest friends, R.O. Morris, Geoffrey Toye, F.B. Ellis, and George Butterworth among them, had already enlisted. Now almost forty-two years of age, flat-footed, and of a decidedly unmilitary bearing (uniform dress was not his strong point: his cap was always crooked, and he could never master the donning of puttees, and always needed help with them) Vaughan Williams was hardly officer material. He joined the Special Constabulary almost immediately, before enlisting as an orderly in the Royal Army Medical Corps, in the 2/4 Field Ambulance detachment.

His first billet, the Duke of York's Barracks in Chelsea, provided new recruits with military education, and basic medical training was given at Guy's Hospital. Ralph attended lectures and worked diligently. Required to observe surgery, he heard the operating physician ask if he had ever seen the inside of a human stomach. Vaughan Williams explained that his usual occupation did not afford such opportunities, whereupon the obliging surgeon promptly enlarged the patient's gaping abdominal incision a further six inches, and proudly displayed its contents to the astonished composer. 'There you are,' he said triumphantly: 'Thank you sir', Ralph replied, so sickened by the grotesqueries of this charnel house that he could muster no other response.

On New Year's Day 1915, his unit relocated to Dorking, but Vaughan Williams was unable to carry out his duties as Ambulance Orderly, for as yet no wagons or horses had arrived. Instead, there followed a gruelling round of route-marches, parades, and stretcher-drills. The unit rose at 4.00a.m. one bitterly cold February morning, and marched to parade at Epsom before General Kitchener. The men stood to attention in blizzard conditions for almost three hours, and Ralph remembered that when the great man finally arrived, he strode past his detachment without so much as pausing to inspect it.

When 2/4 Field Ambulance relocated to a hospital camp at Audley End, south of Cambridge, a kindly adjutant saw that Ralph found a billet with a musical household. His comrade Harry Steggles played the harmonica, and a certain Private Edwards, who had sung in Music Hall shows at the Palladium, formed the nucleus of musical life at camp, but now his host Mr. Machray and his family added their skills on the viola, clarinet, and piano. In rare moments of freedom, Ralph practised on the organ of Bishop's Stortford Parish Church, and impromptu musical evenings took place almost every Saturday at the Machray's. Always eager to contribute to the divisional entertainments at camp, Vaughan Williams and his makeshift 'band' often joined Private Edwards in Music Hall medleys, and their version of *'When Father papered the parlour'* invariably brought the house down.

But Vaughan Williams's darkest presentiments emerged clearly from his writings and letters. He wrote to Gustav Holst shortly before his embarkation for France on 21 June 1916: 'We are on the move, all packed and ready . . . I can't say more. I feel that perhaps after the war England will be a *better* place than it was before. . . . We don't take music as part of our everyday life half enough.' Within weeks of his arrival in what remained of the town of Ecoives, Ralph had seen at first hand the fruits of catastrophe, ferrying desperately wounded soldiers from the trenches to the field dressing station. That he had reached a nadir of despair is clear from his next letter to Holst:

> *I sometimes dread coming back to normal life with so many gaps – especially of course George Butterworth . . . and now I hear that Ellis is killed. Out of those 7 who joined in August 1914 only three are left . . . but then there is always you and thank heaven we have never got out of touch, and I don't see why we ever should.*

In December 1916, the unit moved to a village near Abbeville, and it was assumed that 2/4 Field Ambulance would see service on the Somme. In the event, the men were on the first leg of the journey that would take them to Marseille, and thence by ship to Salonika, where they were stationed on the slopes of Mount Olympus. Vaughan Williams spent the next seven months in Greece, engaged in tasks as varied and stimulating as the repair of mosquito-nets, and latrine duty at 'that God-Forsaken place, Summer Hill Camp'. In January 1918, at the age of forty-five, he received his officer's commission, and returned to spend the final months of his military service in France, in the post of 'Director of Music, B.E.F.'.

He was still stationed at Valenciennes when he received news from London of the death of Sir Hubert Parry, at seventy. His successor as Director of the Royal College of Music, Ralph's friend from Cambridge days, Hugh Allen, was charged with the task of revitalizing the institution after the war. Between 1918 and 1920, Allen recruited some 26 new professors, among them Vaughan Williams and Holst.

Ralph was finally demobilized in February 1919; almost 45 years later, Ursula Vaughan Williams wrote that:

> *Ralph had hated the war, but he had taken part in what he believed had to be done . . . he was going back to a world that lacked many of his friends . . . and to discover how his own invention had survived the years of suppression, wondering whether it could come to life again or whether it was lost for ever, and, if so, what he could do with his life.*

Faced with the prospect of finding a musician to whom he could entrust directorship of the Bach Choir, Hugh Allen (who found himself unable to continue his many conducting engagements due to increasing academic responsibilities in London and Oxford) chose Vaughan Williams as his successor in April 1920. On 19 June, the composer received an Honorary Doctorate in Oxford; Dr. S.A. Godley, the public orator, paid tribute to his services to British music, and in the concert held that afternoon to mark the 250th anniversary of the Sheldonian Theatre, Hugh Allen conducted the Bach Choir for the last time, in a performance of *A London Symphony*.

Ralph's first rehearsal with the Bach Choir was something of a baptism of fire. Diffident and polite by nature, he lacked the extrovert self-assurance of Hugh Allen in marked degree; but unlike his predecessor, Vaughan Williams never showed his annoyance or impatience with the rancour of a martinet, a tendency that Allen never fully overcame. But in remarkably short order, the singers (all of whom were highly experienced amateurs well used to every kind of conductorial vagary) and their new director found the equilibrium needed for a constructive working relationship. As one choir member recalled, Ralph's outsized flat feet, capacious boots and shambling appearance soon endeared him to them, writing that 'as soon as we saw his boots, we knew it would be alright!'

After the cessation of hostilities on the continent, Ralph had returned temporarily to furnished rooms in Sheringham, Norfolk. Although she was now increasingly frail, Adeline had moved there in the hope that the sea air would benefit her invalid brother Hervey, and for Ralph, too, the temporary haven away from Cheyne Walk provided relaxation and new musical stimulus. It was here that he made preliminary sketches for a new orchestral work, the *Pastoral Symphony*, and worked on the opera *Hugh the Drover*. He also prepared a revised version of *A London Symphony*, which received its first performance at the Queen's Hall, on 4 May 1920. In the months that followed, *A London Symphony* would be heard again in the capital, this time under a talented young conductor who was to become one of the greatest exponents of Vaughan Williams's music. His name was Adrian Boult – one of the finest conductors that England has ever produced.

Boult had already risen to prominence before Ralph returned from France, and in February 1919, he had given the premiere of Gustav Holst's best-known work, earning the composer's lasting gratitude for 'having first caused *The Planets* to shine in public'. Many years later, Boult would collaborate with Vaughan Williams in making the first complete recorded traversal of his nine symphonies.

Back at the Royal College of Music, Vaughan Williams earned the affection and respect of students and colleagues alike. The dilapidated Gladstone bag he carried everywhere became as legendary as his own rather novel approach to teaching. Two of his former pupils have left helpful insights into his style and methods. The former, Gordon Jacob writes of his teacher's 'horror of professional skill and technical ability. As he grew older, he came to realize that these qualities did not necessarily add up to a superficial slickness and his later pupils were certainly put through the mill or, as he liked to put it, were "made to do their stodge" methodically.'

In later years at the RCM, Vaughan Williams worried that from time to time, his lessons were too demanding. To one student he said 'I have been concerned that I have been too severe with you . . . will you please take your piece and this note to Mr. Holst?' Unable to contain his curiosity, the unnamed alumnus read these words as he walked down the corridor to Holst's studio: 'Dear Gussie. You know so much more about orchestration than I do. Would you please look at this, and let me know if you think I have been too hard on it. RVW.'

As one of his favourite students, Elizabeth Maconchy, wrote after leaving the College:

> *He had no use for ready-made solutions. He had worked out his own salvation as a composer, and he encouraged his pupils to do the same.*

CHAPTER 6
SERENADE TO MUSIC: YEARS OF GROWING FAME
(1921–38)

- ♦ A Pastoral Symphony
- ♦ The New World
- ♦ First operatic works
- ♦ The White Gates
- ♦ Death of Gustav Holst

The first London performance of Ralph's voluptuously idiomatic tone-portrait for solo violin and orchestra, *The Lark Ascending*, happened on 14 June 1921, with Adrian Boult conducting the British Symphony Orchestra. Vaughan Williams had dedicated the work to the violinist Marie Hall, and this thirteen-minute cameo of the lark in full-throated, ecstatic flight has become one of the composer's most internationally admired creations.

The score had been sketched as early as 1914, but the ensuing European conflict set back both its completion and revision. The piece is not virtuosic in the accepted sense, but is nonetheless technically demanding for the soloist.

The printed score of *The Lark Ascending* is prefaced by these lines from a poem of the same name written by George Meredith (1828–1909); the highly evocative word-painting here makes any further commentary on the music itself superfluous:

> *He rises and begins to round*
> *He drops the silver chain of sound,*
> *Of many links without a break,*
> *In chirrup, whistle, slur and shake.*

For singing till his heaven fills
'Tis love of earth that he instils,
And ever winging up and up,
Our valley is his golden cup,
And he the wine which overflows
To lift us with him as he goes.

Till lost on his aerial rings
In light, and then the fancy sing.

Six months later, Boult directed the premiere of Vaughan Williams's latest full-scale orchestral work (this score also features a part for soprano voice), *A Pastoral Symphony*, at the Royal Philharmonic Society's concert of 26 January 1922. But this deeply personal work with its clear autobiographical associations seemed to many who heard it to be the apogee of that confident, patriotic strain in British music, exampled by Sir Edward Elgar's description of the message that lay behind his own *Symphony No.1 in A flat*; 'great charity – and a massive hope for the future'. Brave words, but for RVW the Great War had changed much that aforetime had seemed fixed and immutable within the English experience. Michael Kennedy has written of 'the emotions of war that are recollected in tranquillity, free from complacency' in *A Pastoral Symphony*. If the work carried any pacifist agenda, it was certainly missed by the critics, and even Hugh Allen felt compelled to write that the piece suggested nothing to him, except perhaps an image of ' . . . VW rolling over and over in a ploughed field on a wet day!'

But here, one finds vivid recollections of the calm after the storm of battle. Quiet forest glades at dusk in the countryside around Ecoives, a bugle-call across distant fields (echoed in a famous solo passage for natural trumpet – Vaughan Williams recalled the time when a brigade musician accidentally sounded the interval of a seventh and not the octave), and the song of a peasant girl that distilled in its innocence the spirit of the balmy summer air. In certain respects, *A Pastoral Symphony* is a nationalistic statement, but one informed by (to quote Kennedy again) 'a visionary, mystical quality, far removed from jingoism or John Bullishness . . . it is Vaughan Williams's *War Requiem*.'

From the start, there was a tremendous divergence of opinion among the press, with the critic of the *Musical Times* calling it 'a dream of sad happiness', and composer Philip Heseltine (better known as Peter Warlock, creator of the *Capriol Suite* for string orchestra) making the infamous observation that to him the music 'seemed like a cow looking over a gate'. By contrast, Gustav Holst rhapsodized over the symphony, writing to the composer 'It's the very essence of you!'

In May, Vaughan Williams set sail for the United States, where he was to conduct *A Pastoral Symphony* at the Summer Festival in Norfolk, Connecticut, in a concert given by the Litchfield County Choral Union. The founding sponsor of the event, the wealthy businessman Carl Stoeckel (his father once held the Chair in Music at Yale) had already managed to sweet-talk Sibelius into making the trip in 1914, and the outdoor 'Music-Shed' in which the festival concerts were staged had been the setting for the first American performance of his tone-poem *The Oceanides*. Ralph and Adeline, who was determined to make the long trip despite her impaired mobility, stayed with the Stoeckels after making land-fall in New York, where the millionaire had booked them a suite at the Plaza Hotel. From here, Vaughan Williams wrote to Holst:

> *I have seen (a) Niagara, (b) the Woolworth building, and am most impressed by (b). I've come to the conclusion that the Works of Man terrify me more than the Works of God ... I've also come to the conclusion that N.Y. is a good place but wants hustling badly(!) – the buses are slow and stop wherever you like. Broadway is, I believe, easier to cross than High Street Thaxted.*

They returned to England after the last concert of the festival on 8 June, arriving home in time for the first performance, at the Royal College of Music on 11 July, of Vaughan Williams's one-act opera *The Shepherds of the Delectable Mountains*. This pastoral episode based on Bunyan's *The Pilgrim's Progress* was heard in public for the first time under the baton of the composer Arthur Bliss. The earliest of Vaughan Williams's works for the stage, much of its material was subsequently incorporated into a full-length opera based on Bunyan's allegory in 1951.

If *The Shepherds* aroused relatively little interest, Vaughan Williams's earliest liturgical work of note, the *Mass in G Minor*, was hailed as a masterpiece of the genre, almost from the day of its first performance in Birmingham Town Hall on 6 December 1922. The correspondent of the *Musical Times* sounded the only negative response when he dubbed the piece 'one of the composer's lesser impulses'. This drew a small but vociferous body of nay-sayers to the cause, which asserted that most of Vaughan Williams's output could be described as 'mock-medieval'. After all, the *Mass* was dedicated to Gustav Holst and his vocal group the Whitsuntide Singers, whose metier was the performance of early polyphonic choral music, mainly from the Tudor period.

Vaughan Williams had also become acquainted with the Master of the Music at Westminster Cathedral Dr. Richard Terry, who reverenced Byrd, Tallis, and Tomkins, but still kept faith with modernism, having conducted the first London performance of Elgar's *The Dream of Gerontius* in 1903. Terry wrote to Vaughan Williams expressing his admiration for the *Mass*: 'I'm quite sincere when I say that it is the work one has all along been waiting for', and later added 'I do very much appreciate the honour that you do us in allowing us to give the first performance of this work. . . .'

But events turned out otherwise, for the City of Birmingham Choir and their director Joseph Lewis introduced the work, leaving Terry with its first liturgical performance on 12 March 1923. In a gesture of loyalty and characteristic integrity, Terry (although deprived of the premiere) continued to champion the *Mass in G Minor* in an article written for the *Cathedral Chronicle* : 'The London press, almost without exception acclaimed the *Mass* as a great work, some critics even going as far as to call it one of the greatest choral works of the century. . . .'

The summer months of 1923 were intensely productive, and the composer's busy schedule became for a time frenetic. Two new works were premiered in barely more than a fortnight. The first, Vaughan Williams's ballet *Old King Cole* (which, to use James Day's lively description 'fills out the pipe, bowl, and fiddlers three of the nursery rhyme with some historical speculation on their origin') was staged under the auspices of Trinity College, Cambridge, on the lawns at Nevile Court on 5 and 7 June. The unpredictable English weather was beneficent for once, and the *Manchester Guardian's* columnist wrote that the ballet 'evoked great enthusiasm. . .' Neither he, nor anyone else who enjoyed the spectacle knew that potential disaster had been only narrowly averted. Ralph was still adding the finishing touches to conductor Boris Ord's manuscript score while the dress rehearsal was under way! The tale of 'King Cole of Colchester', a 'Patron of the Arts who defended his independence against the Romans' is, of course, just happy caprice, but the music is tuneful and lively, and once again, Cambridge had revealed that aspect of Vaughan Williams's creativity in which, to use a term more usually ascribed to Beethoven, we see him in 'Unbuttoned' mood.

Colonel John Sutherland, Commanding Officer at the Royal Military School of Music, Kneller Hall, had thrown down a friendly gauntlet in Vaughan Williams's direction some months before the Cambridge event took place, requesting that he should write something for military band. Ralph was unable to resist the challenge, and on 4 July, Twickenham echoed to the strains of the *English Folksong Suite* when Lieutenant Hector E. Adkins, Director of Music at Kneller Hall conducted the band in the first performance. One buff commented that in this tuneful, ebullient score, Vaughan Williams gave notice that he was 'game to write something for the pier'.

Indeed, it would not be his only composition for military band; its popularity led to a commission for a ceremonial piece for the British Empire Exhibition of 1924, the *Toccata Marziale*. Gordon Jacob, one of Vaughan Williams's students at the RCM supplemented his income as a music copyist, and compiled orchestral and brass band transcriptions of the *English Folksong Suite*, which makes use of nine folk tunes from the composer's vast compendium. The first movement, a brisk march entitled *Seventeen come Sunday* is based on this very tune itself, with '*Dives and Lazarus*' heard in the bass, and intermingled with '*Pretty Caroline*'. The Intermezzo uses '*My Bonny Boy*' and '*Green Bushes*', and the concluding march '*Folksongs from Somerset*' employs no less than four separate melodies; '*Blow away the Morning Dew*', '*High Germany*', '*The Trees so High*', and finally '*John Barleycorn*'.

Vaughan Williams had been contemplating a full-length stage work before World War One; even as far back as the year 1911, he had been making preliminary sketches for what would be his first major opera (or to use his own preferred terminology, a 'Romantic ballad opera') *Hugh the Drover*. The libretto, by Gloucestershire drama critic Harold Child, is a lively pastiche of village life, with its concomitant loves and intrigues mingled with unpretentious gaiety. Yet as the critic and biographer James Day asserts, it does not set out to parallel the human appeal of, say, Smetana's 'village' opera *The Bartered Bride* and probably finds its closest kinship with Benjamin Britten's *Peter Grimes*, in matters of its setting, if not in style.

The scenario devised by Harold Child is a reworking of the classic narrative of the struggle and eventual triumph of true love over the repression of tradition. The heroine of the piece, Mary, is at odds with her father, the village policeman, who has done his best to 'arrange' a match for her with the butcher, John. Mary, meanwhile, has fallen in love with Hugh the Drover, whose bohemian lifestyle is untrammelled by the expectations and demands of village society. The worldly success and prosperity of John the Butcher, meanwhile, has earned him the respect of the populace. After the expected vicissitudes everything turns out right in the end of course; *Hugh the Drover* is operatic pastiche in the best sense of the term – several steps removed from the trivialities of operetta, but rigorous in its exploration of social issues, which it debates with an impressive blend of irony and wit. Between 1910 and 1914, Vaughan Williams reworked the score in detail, and removed one of the most telling lines of the libretto, in which Hugh declared 'I do not love your towns, the smooth sleek life which knows no ups and downs' – sentiments which go some way to conveying in microcosm the sub-text of the entire opera.

The first private performances of *Hugh* were staged at the Parry Opera Theatre of the Royal College of Music, on 9 and 11 July 1924, with S.P. Waddington conducting a student cast and orchestra in a production by Cairns James. The work was presented in public for the first time several days later, when the cast of the British National Opera Company's production (also by Cairns James) took to the stage at His Majesty's Theatre. After a long and demanding season, the principals and chorus were fatigued, and rehearsals, so few as did actually take place, exposed terrifying weaknesses and the woefully under-prepared premiere might well have been a complete fiasco. But the hero of the hour was another rising star of England's conductorial firmament, Malcolm Sargent, who knew the score well, and had been engaged to lead the first professional performances of the opera. Vaughan

Williams later wrote that Sargent 'saved it from disaster every few bars, and pulled chestnuts out of the fire in a miraculous way.' By the end of the performance, first-night catastrophe had been avoided thanks to Sargent's skilled leadership. When called on stage to take his call, Ralph was astonished to see familiar faces of the RCM Chorus sharing the applause; he was told only later that the management had called them in at the very last moment to bolster the professionals, who as yet still barely knew the work!

By the close of the first quarter of the twentieth century, Vaughan Williams had succeeded Elgar as the central figure in British musical life. His works had now been performed as far afield as the United States, at Salzburg, in Venice, Prague, Paris, and at many other major musical centres. His choral setting *Sine Nomine* was even heard in the unlikely and remote surroundings of the island of Patmos (where the Apostle John had written the Book of the Apocalypse) during an Anglo-Catholic Pilgrimage led by Dr. Hutton, Dean of Winchester, and Dr. Russell Wakefield, Bishop of Birmingham. With typically wry humour, Ralph noted in his journal that 'the next visitor to Patmos will probably collect my tune as a folksong!' He also learned that his *Mass in G Minor* was sung regularly in services at the Abbey of Montserrat.

In the ensuing years he was to leave an indelible imprint upon the musical consciousness of a nation no longer quite as sure of itself as it had been in the proud Edwardian era with which Elgar's music had become synonymous. Vaughan Williams was a patriot, certainly, but the national identity he strove to express in his works differed hugely from Elgar's '*Spirit of England*'; he truly sought to give utterance to William Blake's 'Green and pleasant land', although by vastly different means.

That Vaughan Williams produced so many important works in the period 1925–30 was proof positive that British music was still alive and well at a time when revolutionary musical advances were being made on the European mainland. From there, it must have seemed that the music of our islands had lapsed into a kind of isolationist limbo. Today's music historians write volumes concerning the psychological hiatus caused by the seismic after-shocks of radicalism, particularly of the music of the Second Viennese School (Arnold Schoenberg, Alban Berg, and Anton Webern), and of works such as Stravinsky's ballet *Le Sacre du Printemps*. Michael Kennedy writes that:

> *Insularity and a blinkered outlook are the charges frequently
> laid at the door of English music of this period; and Holst and
> Vaughan Williams are misrepresented as though they spent their
> whole life writing variations on* Gathering Peascods. . . .
> *Vaughan Williams never advocated a chauvinistic nationalism –
> he merely urged composers to write the music that they felt was
> in them. . . . In* Flos Campi *and even more in* Sancta Civitas
> *he ploughed a lonely furrow, leaving many of his admirers behind
> and puzzling even such a sympathetic friend as Holst.*

The *Suite for Viola and Orchestra, Flos Campi* (the score also calls for
a small wordless chorus) was heard in London for the first time
at one of Henry Wood's Promenade Concerts on 10 October 1925,
with the great viola virtuoso Lionel Tertis (to whom the work is
dedicated) playing the solo part. *Flos Campi* (orchestral players
lampooned the title as *Camp Flossie*!) was one of the earliest works
to appear during what is often considered the composer's most
productive decade. It is a lavishly exotic work, which abandons
itself to a kind of seductive religious mysticism; the music is
derived from texts in the Song of Solomon, in the Latin Vulgate
version of the Old Testament. Six passages from the writings of
King Solomon are linked together as the basis for the work, and
Vaughan Williams displays an intuitive flair for exotic, oriental
coloration in his handling of the dark sonorities of the viola as it
mingles with the wordless chorus – the music aims to tap the
source of all earthly love.

The work opens with a depiction of the satiated yet ever-un-
fulfilled lover, based on the texts of Chapter I of the Song of
Solomon, and verses 2 and 5:

> *As the lily among thorns, so is my love among thy daughters. . . . Stay
> me with flagons, comfort me with apples; for I am sick of love.*

Of particular interest are sections IV, in praise of Solomon's
mighty men of valour, and VI, 'Set me as a seal upon thine head',
in which the melodic material is unusually similar to the tune *Sine
Nomine*, with which Vaughan Williams seemed eternally fasci-
nated.

Flos Campi came at a time of new self-discovery for Vaughan
Williams, who admitted that he could only muster 'cold admira-

tion' for Holst's new *Choral Symphony* premiered in October 1925. He did, however, write to his friend (Holst was already seriously ill by this point, and was on the verge of what his daughter Imogen called 'that cold region of utter despair') confessing that 'I couldn't bear to think that I was going to drift apart from you musically speaking . . . so I shall live in faith till I have heard it again several times and then I shall find out what a bloody fool I was not to see it all first time.' Holst responded with the comment ' . . . I couldn't get hold of *Flos* a bit and was therefore disappointed with it and me. But I'm not disappointed in *Flos's* composer, because he has not repeated himself.'

Vaughan Williams's *Violin Concerto in D Minor*, also known as the *Concerto Accademico*, a tuneful and attractive work far less popular than it deserves to be, followed hard on the heels of *Flos Campi*, and was heard for the first time at one of Gerald Cooper's concerts at the Aeolian Hall on 6 November. The violinist Jelly d'Aranyi, to whom the concerto is dedicated, took the solo part, joining the string players of Cooper's hand-picked London Chamber Orchestra in a performance that earned enthusiastic critical plaudits. The following evening, *A London Symphony* was heard again in London, with Henry Wood conducting. As Ursula Vaughan Williams wrote in her husband's biography, that November 1925 would have proved 'rather a good month for any composer'.

Another 'difficult' work from the same year was Vaughan Williams's only oratorio *Sancta Civitas* (*The Holy City*); he had planned to use the English form of the title, but had no wish to see his work confused with the parlour-room ballad of the same name. But there were those who saw another opportunity to pillory the composer in the press, since he had expressed publicly his lack of belief in the subject matter he had chosen to set to music, by quoting from Plato's *Phaedo* as a preface to the first printed edition. These lines, with which he chose to illustrate his purpose, are important:

> *Now to assert that these things are exactly as I have described them would not be reasonable. But that these things, or something like them, are true concerning the souls of men and their habitations after death, especially since the soul is shown to be immortal, this seems to me fitting and worth risking to believe.*

> *For the risk is honourable, and a man should sing such things*
> *in the manner of an incantation to himself.*

Ralph's considered reply to his detractors is even more revealing, and here we see (suggests Michael Kennedy) 'why Herbert, Bunyan, Whitman, and even John Bright set his mind alight':

> *There is no form of insincerity more subtle than that which is*
> *coupled with the greatest earnestness of purpose and determination*
> *to do only the best and the highest – this is the unconscious insincerity*
> *which leads us to build up great designs which we cannot fill and*
> *to simulate emotions which we can only feel vicariously.*

The oratorio received its first performance on 7 May 1926 (the fourth day of the General Strike), at an event in Oxford commemorating William Heather's historic proposal (made exactly three hundred years previously) that the University of Oxford should inaugurate a Chair in Music. Writing in *The Times* on 10 May, the music critic H.C. Colles confessed his bewilderment at the work, but at the same time vindicated the composer's own philosophical vision:

> *The disturbance that one feels in listening to the work for the first*
> *time is partly the consciousness that his vision is greater than ours,*
> *and partly a doubt whether he has really chosen the right notes*
> *to convey it to our ears.*

Vaughan Williams resigned his directorship of the Bach Choir in 1928. He was now 56 years old, and he had served the organization faithfully, introducing many new works to British audiences, and raising the technical level of the group to new heights. Composition continued apace, but in the winter months, Ralph was busily correcting proofs for the first edition of the *Oxford Book of Carols*, which he had edited with Martin Shaw. Adeline's health continued to give concern; a fall in October 1927 had resulted in a broken thigh, after which she spent several months in plaster. Honorine Williamson, the young niece of R.O. Morris, joined the household after matriculating in Domestic Science, and was to remain for the next dozen years. In the spring, Adeline was well enough to join Ralph in a rented cottage on the village of Holmbury St. Mary for several weeks, while he added finishing touches to his opera *Sir John in Love*. By common consent, this was not Vaughan Williams's finest stage work, but it is an ingenious and often witty characterization of the tale of Falstaff, even if wholly eclipsed in the public's imagination by Verdi's incomparable masterpiece.

Vaughan Williams knew that such comparison would be inevitable, writing in the preface:

> *To write yet another opera about Falstaff at this time of day may seem to be the height of impertinence, for one appears in doing so to be entering into competition with four great men –* Shakespeare, Verdi, Nicolai *(composer of the operetta* The Merry Wives of Windsor) *and Holst (whose* At the Boar's Head *had proved very successful). . . . My chief object in* Sir John in Love *has been to fit this wonderful comedy with, I trust, not unpleasant music.*

The opera was premiered at London's Royal College of Music under Sargent on 21 March 1929.

The respite from London had afforded the chance to look for a new home in the Dorking area, close to Vaughan Williams's childhood home at Leith Hill Place. Adeline was now too frail to manage the precipitous stairs at 13 Cheyne Walk, and after living at several temporary addresses, the couple finally negotiated the lease of 'Chote Gar', just off the main road to Guildford, in June 1929. They renamed the house 'White Gates'. It would be the composer's home for the remainder of his life, and immediately became the hub of organizational activities for the now flourishing Leith Hill Festival, which Ralph had helped to found many years previously.

Vaughan Williams had begun work on what was to be his finest work for the ballet theatre, *Job – A Masque for Dancing*, in 1927. This massive composition, regarded by some commentators as his greatest creation, takes as its inspiration the Old Testament account of the life of Job, his faith and prosperity, and the tortuous litany of disaster that he endured before the restoration of his fortunes. The original idea for a dance scenario came from Geoffrey Keynes, whose imagination had been fired by the allegorical theatricality of William Blake's illustrations and engravings; Gwen Raverat, another of the Darwin clan, had designed the sets and costumes, but the great Russian choreographer Sergei Diaghilev had declined their invitation to become involved, finding the whole thing 'too English'. Vaughan Williams recognized that the plot offered vast musical possibilities. He loved to read the story of Job in the 1611 King James Version of the Bible, and his enthusiasm for the project did not wane even though he never had the chance to work alongside Diaghilev, who only got to see Blake's dramatic pictures after the score was under way.

The nine scenes of *Job* (Vaughan Williams insisted that it be described as a 'masque' rather than a ballet), depict the pastoral contentment of Job before he and his family are engulfed by a terrifying series of catastrophes; famine, plague, pestilence, sudden death, and fierce battle. After enduring the privation and despair of these trials, in which Job loses his entire substance, he is restored in God's sight to an even greater prosperity than before, but the score also finds room for Job's so-called 'comforters', represented by an important part for saxophone. While it is true that Vaughan Williams's *Job* offers no virtuoso set-pieces for the principal dancers, the combination of (writes James Day) 'the concentrated impact of superb spectacle, magnificent music and a profound theme make *Job* one of the most irresistible aesthetic experiences imaginable.'

The score itself realizes the most potent dramatic images in a series of brilliant creative coups; nowhere is Vaughan Williams's sense of theatre more telling than at that stupendous moment of revelation in which (after receiving the ministrations of the three comforters), Job sees the awful vision of Satan seated upon the throne of the Almighty; the concert version of the work reinforces the texture at this point with a massive organ part. Another notable moment comes when '*All the Sons of God shout for joy*' as Job recovers his own spirituality, celebrated in the beautiful '*Galliard of the Sons of the Morning*'. Finally Satan is repulsed – '*The Lord blessed the latter end of Job more than his beginning*', and the work ends as it began, as Job lives again to dwell in the land. He gazes over the distant cornfields, and blesses his children.

In the autumn of 1932, Vaughan Williams embarked on a second transatlantic voyage, this time to undertake a series of lecturing engagements at the University of Bryn Mawr, Pennsylvania, under the auspices of the Mary Flexner Trust. He delivered six papers, which were collected and published in the volume *National Music*, in 1934. He also journeyed to Boston at the invitation of the Music Director of the Boston Symphony Orchestra, Serge Koussevitzky. At Boston's famous Symphony Hall, Koussevitzky and the orchestra performed the *Tallis Fantasia* in Ralph's honour, but for two matronly Bostonian socialites, the event did not go off quite as expected. They glanced disdainfully at the bulky, shabbily-attired Philistine ensconced at the end of their row of the stalls, and were exasperated by his habit of rising and falling in his seat with every nuance of the music. Sadly, their reaction upon seeing this undignified impostor called to share the applause on stage with the performers was not recorded.

Sir Edward Elgar died at the age of 76, on 23 February 1934. Gustav Holst, already gravely ill, worsened rapidly during a visit to Harvard University, and was forced to return to England, where he died on 25 May. His passing affected Vaughan Williams deeply, for a circle of friendship, which had bonded the pair together closely since student days, was suddenly broken. Writing to Holst's widow and daughter on the eve of his funeral, held at Chichester Cathedral on Midsummer Day 1934, Ralph expressed his sorrow and loss in touchingly intimate terms; 'My only thought is now whichever way I turn, what are we to do without him? – everything seems to have turned back to him – what would Gustav think or advise or do?' Several days after the service, Ralph cut his foot while wandering disconsolately along a Sussex shore, contracted a serious infection, and was confined to bed for the next eight weeks.

In September, now fully restored to health, Vaughan Williams conducted the BBC Symphony Orchestra in a concert at the Queen's Hall, and gave the world the work that has become his international calling-card, the delightful *Fantasia on 'Greensleeves'*, a melody adapted from the opera *Sir John in Love*, and scored for strings, flutes, and harp. The contrasting middle section uses the folk-song *'Lovely Joan '*. But earlier in the year, Adrian Boult and the BBC Symphony Orchestra had introduced another work at this venerable concert room, one made of altogether sterner stuff, Vaughan Williams's electrifying and cataclysmically powerful *Symphony No.4 in F Minor*. This was his first symphony to be identified by a number alone, but its vitriolic angst and destructive power render any extra-musical synonym redundant. The new symphony sounded (to those who would listen) its own threatening alarum, and as Frank Howes observed 'the prophet sees the nature of naked violence triumphant in Europe', adding that in the *Symphony No.6*, too, 'there is similarly a prophetic warning of what will happen to mankind if it persists in its foolish, wicked wars.' But in reality, the impetus behind the piece was altogether more benign, for as Ursula later remembered, Ralph had been amused by a press report of a new work presented at what he liked to call a 'Freak Festival' of new music by anonymous, angry young men – 'So, without any philosophical, prophetic, or political germ, No.4 took its life from a paragraph in *The Times*!'

But we should not set too much store by this account; that this formidable work was the result of some shattering, truly visionary impulse, is beyond question. The manic ferocity of the composer's own vision of the music could be judged from his own commercial recording, made in 1937, but his *Fourth Symphony*, for all its threatening malevolence, spawned one of the best stories of Vaughan Williams the conductor. During a taxing rehearsal session, a player asked him about one particular note, quite certain – from the unorthodox, clashing harmonies resulting when he played the printed notes – that he had discovered a mistake in his part. The bespectacled composer scanned his score professorially, before making this classic riposte: 'Well now, I think it's a B flat . . . I know it looks wrong – it even *sounds* wrong – but it's definitely *right*!'

Two new operas, *The Poisoned Kiss* (or *The Empress and the Necromancer – a 'Romantic Extravaganza'*) and the one-act *Riders to the Sea* emerged in 1936–37. The splendid *Dona nobis pacem* was heard in Huddersfield on 12 October 1936, and this was followed by an aptly ceremonial work for the coronation of King George VI at Westminster Abbey on 12 May 1937.

But the work which seemed, perhaps above all others, to be the spiritual sum of this most productive period of the composer's life was his *Serenade to Music*, written to honour Sir Henry Wood's golden jubilee, and premiered at one of his promenade concerts on 5 October 1938. Vaughan Williams scored the work for orchestra and no fewer than sixteen vocal soloists; each singer involved in the first performance had enjoyed a long professional association with Sir Henry. The texts, taken from Shakespeare's *The*

Merchant of Venice (Act V, scene 1), pay homage to the beauty and power of the noble art of music.

The piece retains its universal appeal, and is unquestionably one of Vaughan Williams's most sublimely compelling scores. Two days after the nation paid tribute to Wood, who had worked tirelessly to revitalize England's musical life in the preceding half-century, the great conductor wrote to the composer, offering these simple tokens of gratitude and admiration:

> *We are so excited to hear from Columbia that they are going to record it.... Again, please accept my warmest and deepest thanks for the* Serenade. *It did raise my Jubilee concert out of the ordinary rut, and lent great distinction to Part I...*

CHAPTER 7
A COMPOSER AT WAR
(1939–45)

♦ *Anxious months – desperate measures*
♦ *A late-night telephone call . . .*
♦ *Films of the war years*
♦ *Symphonies in time of war*

Gaumont British Pictures, Pathe News, Gainsborough, Strand Films and The Crown Film Unit – such names as these continue to evoke stirring images of the mingled patriotism and propaganda that helped to steel public resolve and national pride during the dark years of World War Two. It was the era of gifted, sometimes even great, but more often than not simply unsung heroes of the British cinema industry. Talented directors and producers like Michael Balcon, Anthony Asquith and Ian Dalrymple created a succession of wartime movies that seem now to portray the spirit of the era with almost palpable accuracy. At least, that's how it often seems to those of us who had the good fortune not to have lived through it.

And then there was the music. Written by composers such as Arthur Bliss, Eric Coates, Malcolm Arnold, and many lesser-known figures, majestic and often tear-jerking scores were completed at breakneck speed, and recorded, in countless instances, under the conductor Muir Mathieson, one of Vaughan Williams's former students at the RCM.

Although he was unaware of it at the time, the beginning of hostilities was to signal another phase in Vaughan Williams's creative life. Throughout the tense months of waiting during the autumn of 1939, he searched constantly to find new ways – any ways, no matter trivial they seemed – to serve his country. He contacted the local council offices, offering the parcel of land beside White Gates as a public vegetable allotment, and wrote to a friend in September 'we shall probably be living on potatoes next year – so I'm digging some of my field into a potato patch – it makes me nice and sleepy at night!' He helped with the construction of an air-raid shelter, dug out of the steep grassy bank that divided White Gates from the adjoining house and, when the threat of German raids on London prompted mass evacuation of children from the capital, he and Adeline offered a home to the daughter of his old comrade Harry Steggles. But the child soon became homesick, and Adeline wrote 'Our little girl evacuee Myrtle ordered her parents to fetch her home – that was done yesterday and we have to confess failure.' Ralph worked tirelessly, assisting the Dorking Refugee Committee, and salvaging everything that could be recycled in the war effort. He even assisted local refuse men, as they sifted through mountains of discarded tin cans, rags, paper, rubber, and wood, and then ran a door-to-door War Bonds collection in the evenings.

Vaughan Williams was also a prime mover in staging Dame Myra Hess's famous series of chamber music concerts at the National Gallery; these recitals provided another indelible image of a nation at war. In a quiet moment, he confided to a friend that 'all good things men try to do perish . . . but nothing can destroy music.' Whenever possible, his lecturing commitments continued, and he wrote numerous articles on such subjects as 'Making your own music' and 'The Composer in Wartime', although a projected morale-boosting Leith Hill Festival performance of Beethoven's *Choral Symphony* was abandoned.

Vaughan Williams had always enjoyed occasional visits to the cinema, although he believed that the medium had been underexploited. On one occasion, when faced with the tedious prospect of having to sit through a Three Choirs Festival performance of a monotonous work for which he cared little, he turned to Myra Hess, whispering conspiratorially 'Do you *really* want to hear this . . . let's go to the pictures instead!' He had already hinted to the composer Arthur Benjamin that he 'wouldn't mind a shot at writing for the films', and when he received a telephone call late one Saturday evening towards the end of 1940, he had his chance at last.

Muir Mathieson, now Director of Music for London Films,

asked him to compose the score for a new spy adventure to be set in Canada – *The 49th Parallel*; not unreasonably, Ralph asked how long he might have to finish the task, and received the reply 'till Wednesday, if that's alright'.

Though at first shaken by the impossible deadlines and split-second timings demanded by the film industry, Vaughan Williams was not easily deterred, and in his essay and subsequent radio broadcast 'Composing for the Films' stated that 'when the hand is lazy, the mind often gets lazy as well. A film producer would make short work of Mahler's interminable codas or Dvořák's five endings to each movement', and concluded that the role of the film composer was, in simple terms, 'to ignore the details and intensify the spirit of the whole situation by a continuous stream of music.' He was also keen to stress that successful cinema is the result of a very high degree of co-operation between a number of disciplines, script-writer, cinephotographer, producer, director, actors, and composer, and emphasized the point that 'only when this is achieved will film come into its own as one of the finest of the fine arts.'

The 49th Parallel was the earliest film production to feature Vaughan Williams's music; produced and directed by Michael Powell for Ortus Films, it was screened for the first time in October 1941 at the Odeon, Leicester Square. The cast list was impressive, and included Leslie Howard, Eric Portman, Laurence Olivier, Glynis Johns and Anton Walbrook. The plot concerned the activities of a group of Germans who attempt to subvert and undermine the morale of the people of a remote community on the Hudson Bay, and although somewhat dated by today's standards, it still merits attention, for much of the acting is superb. Vaughan Williams's score, recorded by the London Symphony Orchestra under Muir Mathieson, includes the stirring prelude later set as the hymn '*The New Commonwealth*', with words by Harold Child.

Ian Dalrymple's Crown Film Unit production *Coastal Command* followed in 1942, and this cinematic epitome of wartime propaganda presented to the public gripping visual images of the valour of maritime flyers, and the aircraft they flew, often in situations of great danger. The music follows nighttime sorties from a lonely Hebridean air base, and the exploits of the crews of the Hudsons, Beauforts, and Sunderlands of Coastal Command,

and their skirmishes with German U-Boats and Junkers 88 bombers. The screenings, first at the Plaza, Piccadilly Circus, and then on general release, also brought before the public an ensemble calling itself the RAF Symphony Orchestra, whose ranks included many of the finest orchestral players in the land, assembled to record and perform during the war years; Muir Mathieson again conducted and arranged a concert suite of seven movements from this inspiring score.

The People's Land, first shown privately at the Ministry of Information in March 1943, examined the work of the National Trust. The music, which consisted almost entirely (and by no means inappropriately) of arrangements of English folk-songs, seems to have been sketched several years earlier. The composer's long-standing assistant Roy Douglas recalled being handed several spools of film-takes while working at Elstree Studios in September 1942, on which he discovered unused material later used in another propagandist movie, *The Young Farmers*. Vaughan Williams composed two further cinema scores during the war years. Filippo del Giudice's Two Cities film *The Flemish Farm* concerned the unlikely account of the recovery, by the Belgian Squadron of the RAF, of a Belgian flag left hidden in a field. The only point of note is that the music contained several motifs that provided germinal ideas when the composer came to write his *Symphony No.6* in the years 1944–47.

The Ministry of Information's producer and director Hans Nieter made *The Stricken Peninsula* in 1944, on behalf of the Department of Psychological Warfare. The film documented the involvement of Allied Forces in Naples, but was never shown on general release. The score, which has not survived, apparently included local melodies played by a Neapolitan brass band, who also appeared on the film.

Of the three principal works for the concert hall written during the war years, two were symphonies. The other, the rhapsodically bewitching *Concerto for Oboe and Strings*, a work which, like the *Fifth Symphony*, evoked a lost age of pastoral beauty and innocence, was written for the oboe virtuoso Leon Goossens, and was performed for the first time at Liverpool's Philharmonic Hall on 30 September 1944.

The two wartime symphonies present diametrically polarized aspects of the composer's creative personality, and both are significant milestones in his symphonic output. Vaughan Williams worked intermittently on the score of his *Symphony No.5 in D major* between the years 1938 and 1943. To those who remembered the eruptive vehemence of the prophetic *Symphony No.4* nine years earlier, the premiere of the new symphony under the composer's direction at a Promenade Concert on 24 June 1943 was no less provocative in its effect. Far from being predictive of catastrophe, the *Fifth* is rooted in the benign ethos of some long-lost Bunyanesque medieval Albion. Many saw the new work as emblematic of a deeper spiritual quest for benediction – absolution even – for previous sins of a nation and its people.

Indeed, it would be idle to suggest that the *Fifth Symphony* is anything other than an essay in creative catharsis. The emotional axis of this, one of the greatest of all English compositions in the genre, is the profoundly moving slow movement (*Romanza*) with its haunting cor anglais solo. The score carries an epigraph from Bunyan's *Pilgrim's Progress* which seems singularly apt:

> *Upon this place stood a cross, and below, a little sepulchre. Then he said* 'He hath given me rest by his sorrow, and life by his death.'

Vaughan Williams's *Symphony No.6 in E Minor* was begun against the backdrop of the torment of conflict, in the year 1944. Although of shorter gestation than its predecessor, the work was not heard until 21 April 1948, at a BBC Symphony Orchestra concert conducted by Sir Adrian Boult at the Royal Albert Hall. In every sense, this shocking work is the complete antithesis of the *Fifth*; in it, the critics noted a message of grim catastrophe and violence which outstripped all expectations in its monstrous inevitability. Among those who attended the premiere was the eminent musicologist Deryck Cooke. The following account, taken from his study *The Language of Music*, recalls the overwhelming effect produced by that first hearing, and evinces the malevolent character of the work with disconcerting accuracy. In Cooke's view, the new symphony was . . .

> *. . . nothing short of cataclysmic; the violence of the opening and the turmoil of the first movement; the sinister mutterings of the slow movement, with that almost unbearable passage in which the*

> *trumpets and drums batter out an ominous rhythm, louder and louder, which will not leave off; the vociferous uproar of the Scherzo and the grotesque triviality of the Trio; and most of all, the slow finale, pianissimo throughout, devoid of all warmth and life, a hopeless wandering through a dead world ending literally in* niente *– nothingness.*
>
> *This at any rate was my impression while the music was being played. I remember my attention was distracted, near the end, by the unbelievable sight of a lady powdering her nose – one wondered whether it was incomprehension, imperviousness, or a defence mechanism . . . I was no more able to applaud than at the end of Tchaikovsky's* 'Pathétique'. *Less so, in fact, for this seemed to be an ultimate nihilism beyond Tchaikovsky's conceiving – every drop of blood seemed frozen in one's veins.*

The broadly expansive E major theme at the close of the first movement, a fleeting vision of hope and fragile assurance amid the storm, was used (and as I recall, to powerfully idiomatic effect), as the theme for the 1970s television series *A Family at War*.

Vaughan Williams retained his contact with the film industry after World War Two, and indeed throughout the remaining years of his career. With the British film industry's postwar revitalization, he was commissioned to write the score for Michael Balcon's *The Loves of Joanna Godden* in 1947. The following year brought his finest contribution to the medium – an outstanding score for Balcon's Ealing Studios classic, *Scott of the Antarctic*. His last film score dates from 1955, and was written for the British Transport Commission's *The England of Elizabeth*.

But the creative impulse behind Vaughan Williams's film music can be traced back to the harrowing and anxious days of 1940, when he publicly expressed his views on the role of music, and of the composer in time of trial, during a famous BBC radio broadcast. He asked his listeners to consider the social as well as political function of the arts, in this oft-quoted line from 'The Composer in Wartime', in which he threw down the challenge to those who claimed that in times of strife, national priorities lay elsewhere:

> *Are there not ways in which the composer, without derogating his art, without being untrue to himself, but still without that*

entire disregard for his fellows which characterizes the artist in supreme moments, use all his skill, his knowledge, his sense of beauty in the service of his fellow men?

Ralph Vaughan Williams, perhaps more than those of his creative contemporaries who lived and worked in cloistered isolation, had laboured hard to make it so.

CHAPTER 8
THANKSGIVING FOR VICTORY . . . THE FINAL YEARS (1945–58)

The closing chapters of a long and distinguished career reveal a very different Vaughan Williams, grandee of English music, and recognized as a master, not just by the world at large, but also (and with all the touching modesty and self-deprecation that was the man) by the composer himself. His final years were musically productive, yet not wholly untroubled by the sadnesses that accompany increasing age. By the end of World War Two, Vaughan Williams had reached the age of 73, yet the fact that he still very much retained the 'common touch' was shown in a major work commissioned by the BBC when Allied victory was at last in sight. *A Thanksgiving for Victory* (for speaker, chorus, and orchestra) was first broadcast to mark the German surrender on 13 May 1945. Probably no other work by Vaughan Williams ever captured the national mood quite so eloquently; the texts came variously from the Bible, Shakespeare's *Henry V* (Act IV, scene 8), and from

Kipling's *Puck of Pook's Hill*. The work was heard at a Promenade Concert (now relocated to the Royal Albert Hall, following the destruction of the Queen's Hall in the Blitz) on 14 September, under the revised title *A Song of Thanksgiving*.

The famous sculptor Sir Jacob Epstein, who crafted a fine bronze bust of the composer, left the following description of him, based on numerous 'sittings', after one of which he received an invitation to attend a performance of Bach's *St Matthew Passion*. Epstein later described the profound effect that occasion had upon him, but here are his impressions of Vaughan Williams, founded upon the many hours of conversation that took place between them in the sculptor's studio:

> *Here was the master with whom no one could venture to dispute. He reminded one in appearance of some eighteenth-century admiral whose word was law. Notwithstanding I found him the epitome of courtesy and consideration, and I was impressed by the logic and acuteness of everything he discoursed upon and was made aware of his devotion to an art as demanding as sculpture.*

In March 1946, Vaughan Williams attended the Wigmore Hall premiere of another significant instrumental work, alas all too infrequently performed today, the *Introduction and fugue* for two pianos, written especially for the famous British keyboard partnership of Phyllis Sellick and Cyril Smith. The *Sixth Symphony* was now almost complete, and it was one the first major orchestral works in which Vaughan Williams's assistant and copyist Michael Mullinar had been actively involved. Both Mullinar and his successor in the job, Roy Douglas, have commented on the perils of the tasks set before them; the composer's drafts were sometimes an illegible mass of scribblings out and (writes Douglas) 'here and there a page, or line would be stuck slightly askew over the original copy, and an extra bar added in some corner with an arrow pointing to it.' Vaughan Williams, who relied increasingly upon Roy Douglas in later years, and regarded him as a trusted friend whose judgement was often sought over questions of orchestration when any new work was 'ready to have its face washed', always took vicarious pleasure in introducing him to friends as 'the man who writes my music'.

As elder-statesman of England's musical heritage, Ralph was

also in demand as a conductor of his own works, and he attained what many still remember as his finest hour on the podium on the evening of 21 July 1946, when he directed a live 'Prom' broadcast of *A London Symphony*. Adeline's diary wrote that it was:

> *R's great day with the London Symphony Orchestra – he was off at 8 for 10'0'c rehearsal – and will be back at 1 0'c for lunch – then an afternoon sleep, dress, and tea at 5, and off again by 6 and home at 10. I shall be glad when it is over as always, but he is in good fettle, and really knows the* London; *the weather is much better than yesterday* . . .

He was again at the conductor's desk on 12 September (*Symphony No.5*), and on 6 November, when he again led *A London Symphony* at the Albert Hall. During the reception afterwards at The Dorchester, he was able to break a habit imposed by wartime, and after the meal enjoyed his first cigar in years; but having imbibed a little too liberally of the champagne and post-concert cocktails, he managed to let the ignited cigar fall under the adjoining seat, occupied by a young, beautiful, and voluminously-petticoated debutante. 'What am I to do . . . let her burn alive, or dive under her petticoats?' – an observant waiter saved the day, though apparently not a moment too soon.

In 1948, Vaughan Williams started work on his opera *The Pilgrim's Progress*. Long in the making, it would be his last, and certainly his greatest exploration of the medium, though not for the first time, he was publicly ambivalent about the semantic inferences of the term 'Opera', and chose to describe the work as 'A Morality, in a Prologue, four Acts, and an Epilogue, founded on John Bunyan's Allegory of the same name.' This massive score, which involves 34 soloists (although many parts can be doubled), chorus, and orchestra, incorporates passages from the earlier Bunyan stage work, *The Shepherds of the Delectable Mountains*. The scenario is divided into individual tableaux, presenting different stages in Pilgrim's journey, and charting his progress through the snares of worldly concerns, the battles with Appollyon, to his final attainment of the Heavenly City.

Vaughan Williams completed the score in the first weeks of 1951, and it was presented at Covent Garden on 26 April. Ursula Vaughan Williams described the anxious days before the premiere in graphic detail: '. . . there were very few of his friends he wanted to see until it was over. . . . I had experienced the prolonged agony before a performance several times . . . I understood how fearful this culmination of years of intense work translating vision into music and drama must be for the composer.' Yet for Vaughan Williams, the fears were altogether more deep-seated, and could not be set at nought by superb singing, magnificent production, and brilliant sets. The fact remained that *Pilgrim* was the most radical departure away from perceived operatic convention that he had ever attempted, and he feared the response of the critics: 'They won't like it, they don't want an opera with no heroine and no love duets . . . I don't care, it's what I meant, and there it is.' The next morning's papers confirmed his prediction, and Vaughan Williams's most ambitious stage work was received with the kind of muted, but respectful interest that might best be described as 'damning with faint praise'.

When, four years previously, Ernest Irving asked him to write the score for a new Ealing Films adventure based on Captain Scott's ill-fated attempt to reach the South Pole, Vaughan Williams had been reluctant to accept the commission, for *Pilgrim* claimed too much of his time and energies already. Yet Irving was persistent, and after reading an account of Scott's expedition in *The Worst Journey in The World*, Ralph's enthusiasm was fired, and very soon White Gates was filled with strange new sounds, musical depictions of chill polar winds, of vast empty vistas of desolate ice, of eerie light and of cheery penguins and massive whales. But mostly, it was the cavalier heroism, and the inextinguishable human desire to master the natural environment, irrespective of personal cost that inspired Vaughan Williams to produce one of the greatest cinema scores by any British composer.

Hugh Ottaway has written that:

> *The time and the subject were particularly right; the spiritual desolation of the* Sixth Symphony *found its physical counterpart in the polar wastes, and the sense of challenge and endurance in the symphony was re-engaged by the story of Scott's last expedition. Even so, Vaughan Williams's very deep involvement in his Scott music calls for some explanation. This is to be found in the music's human values and in the way these give an 'answer' to the symphony.*

During the years 1949–52, material from the film score was used in the last of Vaughan Williams's named and un-numbered symphonies, the *Sinfonia Antarctica*, a five-movement work for large orchestra, women's chorus, and solo soprano. Dedicated to Ernest Irving, this remarkable work was first heard at Manchester's Free Trade Hall, under Sir John Barbirolli on 14 January 1953. This visionary and unusually impressionistic score, in essence a series of five mood-pictures with accompanying texts from Shelley's *Prometheus Unbound*, from the Book of Psalms ('There go the ships and there is that Leviathan whom thou hast made to make his pastime therein.'), Coleridge, John Donne, and finally from Captain Scott's journal ('I do not regret this journey; we took risks, we knew we took them, things have come out against us, therefore we have no cause for complaint'), and its orchestration includes prominent parts for a range of unusual instruments, including the Wind Machine. The programme suggested by the texts is more contemplative than explicit, yet as Frank Howes wrote after the first performance 'the listener carries away from a hearing of the *Sinfonia* an unspoken moral – the spirit of man facing fearful odds and bravely accepting his loss of the battle.'

After years of crippling ill-health, Adeline Vaughan Williams died peacefully at White Gates on 10 May 1951, at the age of 80; she was buried in the Fisher family's plot in the churchyard at Brockenhurst, Hampshire.

In 1938, Ralph had been introduced to Ursula Wood, widow of a Royal Artillery Officer, Lt.Col. J. Michael J. Forrester-Wood, and had collaborated with her on a masque intended for the English Folk Dance Society. Ursula Wood had supplied texts based on Spenser's *Epithalamion*. In the years that followed, a bond developed between them, founded on mutual respect and propriety, as Ursula continued to offer willing assistance with originating and editing texts for the composer, and was involved particularly with *The Pilgrim's Progress*. Ursula also wrote the verses for a choral work entitled *Silence and Music*, Vaughan Williams's contribution to a unique musical tribute to the new Queen, Elizabeth II, for which ten English composers had been invited to write sections of *A Garland for the Queen*.

The couple were married on 7 February 1953, and in August, following the sale of White Gates, they settled into 10 Hanover Terrace, Regent's Park, which would be Ralph's home for the remaining five years of his life.

Two works for unusual solo instruments and orchestra date from this period, and each deserves mention here. The harmonica-player Larry Adler had asked Vaughan Williams to consider writing something for his instrument, which hitherto had made little impression upon the world of 'serious' music, and on 3 May 1952, Adler played the new *Romance in D Flat* for harmonica, string orchestra, and piano, at the New York Town Hall. In September, Adler performed the work in London, and became the first harmonica-player ever to appear at a Henry Wood 'Prom'. A concert held at the Royal Festival Hall to mark the Golden Jubilee of the London Symphony Orchestra on 13 June 1954, included another new work commissioned especially for the occasion. This was the memorable *Tuba Concerto in F Minor*, which was played by the orchestra's tuba-player, Philip Catelinet, with Sir John Barbirolli conducting. In this unusual composition, the tuba is given an entirely new identity, and is allowed to demonstrate its remarkable agility in the outer movements, and its soulful lyricism in the beautiful *Romanza* that lies at the heart of the work. In his preface to the published edition, Vaughan Williams described the piece as 'nearer to the Bach form than that of the Viennese School (Mozart and Beethoven), although the first and last movements each finish with an elaborate cadenza that allies the concerto with the Mozart–Beethoven form.'

In September 1954, Ralph and Ursula left London for what would be the composer's final visit to the United States. Early in the New Year, they had hosted the baritone Keith Falkner at Hanover Terrace; over lunch, Vaughan Williams lamented that there remained much he had yet to see, mentioning both Rome and the Grand Canyon, at which point Ursula interjected with a reassuring 'Well, why don't you see them both then?' Falkner remained pensive. He had only recently returned to London following a stay in America, and came forward with the suggestion that a lecture tour in the USA would at least afford the chance to visit one of these long-dreamt- of localities.

And so plans were laid for a taxing and intense schedule of talks, lectures, broadcasts and concerts, which might well have made a younger man blanch at the prospect. In the event, the octogenarian composer showed himself to have seemingly inexhaustible reserves of energy, and Ursula noted that while in New

York, he would have insisted on viewing the sunset from the top of the Empire State Building even if the lifts had been out of order! A punishing series of lectures lay ahead, at Cornell and Yale Universities, and transcripts were published in 1955 under the general title *The Making of Music*. He gave composition master classes at major centres, and on one occasion offered an immortal piece of advice to an aspiring student composer who had submitted a movement of a dissonant and complex new work for Vaughan Williams's criticism. 'Well, my boy', he ventured, 'if a tune *should* happen to occur to you, don't hesitate to write it down!'

Vaughan Williams spent his eighty-second birthday at a concert arranged in his honour by the students and faculty of the University of Michigan School of Music. Indiana University had recently performed his *Five Tudor Portraits*, and the couple spent some time on the campus while travelling to California, with the long-awaited diversion en route to view the Grand Canyon. Yale had conferred upon him its greatest academic honour, the Howland Memorial Prize, and Vaughan Williams had been nominated as the outstanding musical personality of the year by the National Arts Foundation of America; the citation described him as a 'Miltonic figure', whose music was 'full of splendour without tinsel'.

Vaughan Williams lived to complete nine symphonies, attaining to that magical numeric benchmark of completeness prescribed by Beethoven, and perpetuated by Schubert, Dvořák, Bruckner, and Mahler. The *Eighth Symphony* (1953–55), scored for a Schubertian orchestra with harp and added percussion, is the most genial and transparent of the series. It is also the most imaginatively scored, having an opening movement described by the composer as 'Seven Variations in search of a Theme', and a virile, life-asserting final *Toccata* in which, writes Hugh Ottaway, 'Youth and age are one.'

The *Ninth Symphony*, premiered at the Royal Festival Hall on 2 April 1958, under Sir Malcolm Sargent, is the work (writes James Day) 'not of a tired old man, but of a very experienced one.' It was Vaughan Williams's last significant composition, but was never conceived (as were Bruckner's and Mahler's *Ninths*) as a valedictory gesture of symphonic farewell. The work advanced an evolution of symphonic thought already explored by its predecessors, and its mood is at once heroically affirmative, and enigmatically resigned. 'There are dark visionings', writes Hugh Ottaway, 'and a sense of struggle against odds is never far away, but the ultimate note, as in the *Eighth*, is one of qualified optimism.'

The score of Vaughan Williams's *Ninth Symphony* includes parts for a trio of saxophones, and a part for flügelhorn. The introduction to the printed score includes the explanation that 'this beautiful and neglected instrument is not usually allowed in the select circles of the orchestra and has been banished to the brass band, where it is allowed to indulge in its bad habit of vibrato to its heart's content. While in the orchestra it will be expected to sit up and play straight. The Saxophones, also, are not expected, except possibly in one place in the *Scherzo*, to behave like demented cats, but are allowed to be their own romantic selves. . . .' Perhaps this joviality concealed in part the composer's innermost concern that this symphony would, perhaps, be his last. If so, then Michael Kennedy's assessment of the piece is unusually poignant; 'It would be wrong to read an elegiac intent into this symphony; rather is it as if he was opening a new chapter. Vaughan Williams, eschewing sentimentality, for the last time summons up those reserves which, for want of a better word, must be called visionary.'

Ralph Vaughan Williams died peacefully and unexpectedly at his home on the morning of 26 August 1958, at the age of eighty-five, with natural causes the likely culprit. Not even the trauma of undergoing surgery during the previous September had robbed him of his insatiable zest for life, and his boundless enthusiasm for a huge variety of projects, both musical and otherwise, seemed undiminished. He was, at the time of his passing, a national figure, universally loved and admired as a man of genius, and as a human being who seemed profoundly and singularly untainted by his success. He continued to work right to the end; on the day he died, he had been due to journey across London to Walthamstow Town Hall, where Sir Adrian Boult and the London Philharmonic were recording the *Ninth Symphony* as the last instalment in a complete cycle of his symphonies for the gramophone, on the Decca label.

The funeral service took place at Westminster Abbey on 19 September and, in accordance with his own request, the choir sang Maurice Greene's great anthem *Lord let me know mine end*. Among the composer's own music performed that day was the *Pavane of the Sons of the Morning*, from *Job*.

Ralph Vaughan Williams had served his art, his country, and above all, his fellow men and women, whose own lives had been enriched beyond measure by his own charm, humility, and integrity of purpose. That he managed to retain his own Kiplingesque 'common touch', amid the harsh, disjunctive clamour of musical modernism, ensured that he realized that most precious of all creative ideals. Vaughan Williams succeeded where countless others have failed, and continue to fail – all his compositions, regardless of style, genre or content, have this in common: they are at once both meaningful and accessible to the broadest cross-section of music-lovers. That selfless legacy lives on still in his music, and gives to any who would listen a glimpse of that untroubled Albion for which he had striven long and mightily all his life.

CHAPTER 9
VAUGHAN WILLIAMS ON DISC

The orchestral, chamber, and vocal works of Ralph Vaughan Williams receive extensive coverage in the current record catalogues, and the breadth of releases encompassing all price brackets should enable even the most cash-conscious collector to assemble a good cross-section of the composer's music with little difficulty. There remains, however, a pronounced dearth of recordings of the composer's stage works, and inevitably some of his operas have so far failed to find substantial representation on compact disc.

The following 'essential' recordings have been selected on the basis of their artistic strengths alone, although in many cases it will be possible to obtain more than one key work on the same issue. By careful selection, the collector can avoid unnecessary duplication of titles, and in some instances, budget or mid-price discs, sometimes consisting of reissued material, will prove to be the finest option. Inevitably, however, the most recent recordings offer the finest technological advances in sound engineering, and for those who possess high-quality playback equipment, the advantages will be readily apparent, although these discs are usually available only in the higher price brackets.

The late Bryden Thomson was one of those rare conductors who had the full measure of *A Sea Symphony*; his spectacular recording of the work (⊗ Chandos 8764) features magnificent solo singing from soprano Yvonne Kenny and baritone Brian Rayner Cook, both of whom sound nobly assured in the Whitman texts. The London Symphony Orchestra and Chorus provide a spectacular aural backdrop to this definitive account.

André Previn recorded *A London Symphony* for the American audiophile label Telarc in 1987 (⊗ Telarc CD-80138); it remains an altogether outstanding performance, with stunning dynamic range and pin-sharp orchestral detailing. This issue comes at full price, but I'd commend it in the strongest possible terms as being worth every penny! The orchestra is the Royal Philharmonic, whose leader at the time was Barry Griffiths, who completes the disc as violin soloist in a yearningly beautiful reading of *The Lark Ascending*. It is one of those comparatively rare recordings in which everything seems to go well, and I cannot imagine the piece being better served by any rival performance.

The mid-priced EMI Eminence label has issued a fine integral survey of Vaughan Williams's symphonies, complete with his *Serenade to Music*, performed by the Royal Liverpool Philharmonic Orchestra and Chorus under Vernon Handley, always one of the most consistently rewarding interpreters of RVW's music. Those who splash out on the complete 6-disc set (⊗ EMI Eminence CD BOX VW1) will not be disappointed, although Handley's enraptured reading of the *Symphony No.5* coupled with the *Flos Campi* suite (⊗ EMI Eminence CD-EMX 9512) is a self-commending highlight and represents faithfully the impressive virtues of Handley's series. Try it first if you have any reservations about buying the whole set.

Teldec's British Line series, with Andrew Davis and the BBC Symphony Orchestra, features superior recorded sound and momentous performances, never bettered, I think, than by Davis's remarkably objective traversal of Vaughan Williams's *Symphony No.6* (⊗ Teldec British Line 9031 - 73127-2). This shattering interpretation brings world-class playing from the BBC Symphony Orchestra; the coupling – a warmly focussed version of the *Fantasia on a Theme of Thomas Tallis* – is equally memorable, and the disc concludes with violinist Tasmin Little's ethereal realization of *The Lark Ascending*.

At full price, Bernard Haitink's unmissable performance of the *Sinfonia Antarctica*, with the London Philharmonic Orchestra and Choir, and soprano soloist Sheila Armstrong, is unquestionably authoritative. Haitink charts his course through these five movements with unerring skill, and one is left with powerful images of the human struggle against merciless and hostile natural forces; the recorded sound is appropriately visceral and detailed (⊗ EMI CDC7 47516-2).

The American conductor Leonard Slatkin seems to have a

natural affinity with British music, and his coupling of Vaughan Williams's *Symphonies Nos.8 & 9*, with the Philharmonia Orchestra (⊗ RCA Victor Red Seal 09026 61196-2) claims an emphatic prime recommendation for these works.

One of the finest of all modern versions of *Job – a Masque for Dancing* comes from Richard Hickox and the Bournemouth Symphony Orchestra in the critically-acclaimed EMI British Composers series (⊗ EMI CDC 7 54421-2). I'd hesitate to part with this issue, and would happily pay twice the asking price for a performance of this quality.

No Vaughan Williams discography is complete without some reference to his wartime film scores, and conductor Andrew Penny has assembled a very serviceable compilation of extracts from *The 49th Parallel*, *Coastal Command*, and *The Flemish Farm* (⊗ Marco Polo 8.223665). The RTE Concert Orchestra plays with commitment and relish, and the disc also includes Vaughan Williams's *Three Portraits from the England of Elizabeth.*

Turning to the world of song, a recent release from Collins Classics (⊗ Collins Classics 14882) brings together a representative selection of highly evocative works spanning over half a century of Vaughan Williams's creative life, in Volume I of the English Song Series. The programme includes superlative performances of *On Wenlock Edge* and the *Five Mystical Songs*, in addition to other Vaughan Williams songs. This inspirational disc is probably the finest introduction to Vaughan Williams's vocal music to emerge for some time, and the performers are the tenor Anthony Rolfe Johnson, baritone Simon Keenlyside, Graham Johnson, piano, and the Duke String Quartet.

From Hyperion comes another praiseworthy disc devoted to Vaughan Williams's vocal music, and centered around a gloriously ripe, radiantly expressive account of the *Serenade to Music*. Matthew Best directs the Corydon Singers, the English Chamber Orchestra, and an impressive roster of soloists (⊗ Hyperion CDA 66420); for good measure, violist Nobuko Imai is outstanding in *Flos Campi*, and the *Fantasia on Christmas Carols* completes a worthy offering from this much-admired label. The same conductor (on ⊗ Hyperion: CDA 66569) also directs admirable performances of *A Song of Thanksgiving*, *Three Choral Hymns*, *The Old Hundredth*, and excerpts from *The Shepherds of the Delectable Mountains*.

Vaughan Williams's complete *String Quartets*, and the seldom heard *Phantasy Quintet*, are expertly played by the members of the English String Quartet with Norbert Blume, viola, on their fine 1988 recording for Unicorn Kanchana (⊗ DKPC CD 9076). Also well worth considering is the interesting juxtaposition of string quartets by Ravel and Vaughan Williams, buffered by an incomparably eloquent and deeply moving version of *On Wenlock Edge* (⊗ EMI CDC7 54346-2). The solo tenor Philip Langridge is joined by the Britten Quartet and pianist Howard Shelley. Were my budget limited to the purchase of just one disc of Vaughan Williams's chamber music, this unusually distinguished EMI offering would have to be the one.

Although Sir Malcolm Sargent's vintage 1924 recording of the opera *Hugh the Drover* is available in Pearl's historical reissues catalogue (⊗ Pearl GEM MCD 9468), with the original cast, a rather better bet is Matthew Best's finely crafted Hyperion performance, which comes on two discs (⊗ CDA 66901-2). However, it is Sir Adrian Boult's classic recording of *The Pilgrim's Progress* that must be regarded as the greatest of all Vaughan Williams's opera performances ever committed to disc. EMI's two-disc set (⊗ EMI CMS7 64212-2) also includes rehearsal sequences.

Collectors with an ear for historical performances should certainly obtain Vaughan Williams's own recording of his *Symphony No.4 in F minor*, recorded in 1938 with the BBC Symphony Orchestra. In a famous remark made during rehearsals, the composer is said to have put down his baton, saying to the orchestra: 'Well gentlemen, if that's modern music, you can have it!' In the event, he secured a galvanic response from his players, and despite its age and the obvious technical limitations of the recording itself, this remains a matchless account of the work. The coupling on this essential Koch International CD (⊗ Koch 37018-2) is Holst's 1926 recording, with the London Symphony Orchestra of his suite *The Planets*.

SUGGESTED
FURTHER READING

Vaughan Williams's life in music has been remarkably well documented. In addition to the standard texts, such as Michael Kennedy's authoritative study of his compositions, the reminiscences of those with whom he enjoyed close family or professional associations provide unique insights into the man behind the music, both as public celebrity and as private creative artist.

Both Ursula Vaughan Williams and Roy Douglas give touching portrayals of the composer's humility and humanity, while Wilfrid Mellers outlines his distinctive artistic ambitions.

Equally, Vaughan Williams's own writings – often as candid and good-humoured as they are insightful, help to round out the picture of a scholarly, dedicated, but essentially human and down-to-earth practical musician.

James Day: *Vaughan Williams* (Dent Master Musicians, 1961)

Roy Douglas: *Working with R.V.W.* (Oxford University Press, 1972)

Michael Kennedy: *The works of Ralph Vaughan Williams* (Oxford University Press, 1964)

Wilfrid Mellers: *Vaughan Williams and the Vision of Albion* (Barrie & Jenkins, 1989)

Hugh Ottaway: *Vaughan Williams Symphonies* (BBC Music Guides, 1972)

Ralph Vaughan Williams: *Some thoughts on Beethoven's Choral Symphony and other writings* (Oxford University Press, 1953)

Ursula Vaughan Williams: *A biography of Ralph Vaughan Williams* (Oxford University Press, 1964)

RALPH VAUGHAN WILLIAMS: COMPLETE LIST OF WORKS

No book of this kind would be complete without a systematic listing of the works of the composer under review. In the case of Ralph Vaughan Williams, the task of compiling a catalogue of his music is a relatively straightforward matter.

In the following pages, the composer's output has been divided into its representative categories, to provide a user-friendly point of reference that will be helpful particularly when used in conjunction with the guide to recommended recordings given in Chapter 9 and the suggestions for further reading on the previous page.

ORCHESTRAL WORKS

Symphonies

A Sea Symphony for soprano and baritone soloists, chorus, and orchestra (1910)
A London Symphony (1913; revised 1918)
Pastoral Symphony for soprano solo and orchestra (1921–22)
Symphony No.4 in F minor (1931–34)
Symphony No.5 in D (1938–43)
Symphony No.6 in E minor (1944–47)
Sinfonia Antarctica (1949–52)
Symphony No.8 in D minor (1953–55)
Symphony No.9 in E minor (1958)

Music for stage and cinema

Incidental music for Aristophanes' *The Wasps* (1909)
Ballet *Old King Cole* (1924)
Job – A Masque for Dancing (1930)
The Running Set (1935)

Film scores

The 49th Parallel (1940)
Coastal Command (1942)
The People's Land (1943)
The Flemish farm (1943)
Stricken Peninsula (1945)
The loves of Joanna Godden (1947)
Scott of the Antarctic (1949)

Miscellaneous orchestral music

Norfolk Rhapsody No.1 (1905)
In The Fen Country (1905; revised 1937)
Fantasia on a Theme of Thomas Tallis (1910; revised 1923)
English Folksong Suite (1923)
Toccata Marziale for military band (1924)
Five Variants on Dives and Lazarus (1939)
Partita for double string orchestra (1948)
Concerto grosso for strings (1950)
Variations for brass band (1957)

Works for solo instruments and orchestra

The Lark Ascending for violin and small orchestra (1914)
Concerto Accademico for violin and strings (1925)
Flos Campi for viola, chorus and small orchestra (1926)
Piano Concerto (1933; transcribed for two pianos and orchestra, 1946)
Suite for viola and small orchestra (1934)
Romance for harmonica, strings, and piano (1953)
Tuba Concerto (1954)

OPERAS AND STAGE WORKS

The Shepherds of the Delectable Mountains (1922)
Hugh the Drover (1924)
Sir John in Love (1929)
Riders to the Sea (1931)
The Poisoned Kiss(1936)
The Pilgrim's Progress (1951)

CHAMBER MUSIC

Phantasy Quintet for strings (1912)
Romance and Pastorale for violin and piano (1923)
String Quartet No.1 in G minor (1924)
Six Studies in English Folksong for cello (or violin, viola or clarinet) and piano (1927)
Household Music (1924)
String Quartet No.2 in A minor ('For Jean, on her Birthday') (1944)
Sonata in A minor for Violin and Piano (1956)

WORKS FOR KEYBOARD

Piano music

Suite of Six Short Pieces (1921; later arranged for string orchestra under the title *Charterhouse Suite*)
Hymn-tune *Prelude on Gibbons' Song 13* (1930)
Canon and *Two-part Invention* (1934)
2 Two-part Inventions (1934)
Valse Lente and *Nocturne* (1934)
The Lake in the Mountains (from the film score *The 49th Parallel*) (1947)
Introduction and Fugue for two pianos (1946)

Organ music

Three Preludes on Welsh Hymn Tunes (1920)
Prelude and Fugue in C minor (1921)

MAJOR CHORAL WORKS

Willow Wood (texts by Dante Gabriel Rossetti) for baritone, female chorus, and orchestra (1903)

Toward the Unknown Region (texts by Walt Whitman) for chorus and orchestra (1905; revised 1918)

Five Mystical Songs (texts by George Herbert) (1911)

Fantasia on Christmas Carols for baritone, chorus, and orchestra (1912)

Mass in G minor (1922–23)

Sancta Civitas oratorio for tenor, baritone, chorus and orchestra (1925)

The 100th Psalm (1929)

Benedicite for soprano, chorus, and orchestra (1930)

Three Choral Hymns (1930)

Magnificat for contralto, female chorus, and orchestra (1932)

Five Tudor Portraits for contralto, baritone, chorus, and orchestra (1936)

Dona nobis pacem for soprano, bass, chorus and orchestra (1936)

Festival Te Deum (1937)

Serenade to Music (1938)

Thanksgiving for Victory for soprano, speaker, chorus and orchestra (1945)

The Sons of Light (1951)

An Oxford Elegy for speaker, chorus and orchestra (1952)

Hodie for soprano, tenor, bass, chorus, organ, and orchestra (1954)

VOCAL WORKS

Works for unaccompanied chorus

Three Elizabethan Part-songs (1891–96)

'*Sound Sleep*' (Christina G. Rossetti) (1903)

'*Rest*' (Christina G. Rossetti) (1905)

'*Ring out, ye bells*' (Sir Philip Sidney) (1905)

'*Fain would I change that Note*' (anon.) (1907)

'*Come Away, Death*' (William Shakespeare) (1909)

'*Love is a sickness*' (Samuel Daniel) (1918)

'*It was a Lover*' (William Shakespeare) (1921)
'*Dirge for Fidele*' (William Shakespeare) (1921)
'*England, my England* ' (William Henley) (1941)
Three Shakespeare Songs (1951)
'*Silence and Music*' (Ursula Wood) (1953)
'*Heart's Music*' (Thomas Campion) (1955)
Songs for a Spring Festival (Ursula Vaughan Williams) (1955)

Anthems

Three Motets (1920–21)
O vos omnes for solo alto and 8-part chorus (1922)
Magnificat and *Nunc Dimitis* (1925)
Te Deum (1928)
'*The Pilgrim Pavement*' (1934)
'*O How Amiable*' (1924)
Morning, Communion and Evening Service (1939)
'*A Hymn of Freedom*' (text by G.W. Briggs) (1939)
Six Choral Songs to be sung in time of war (texts by Percy B. Shelley) (1940)
'*The Airmen's Hymn*' (1942)
'*The Souls of the Righteous*' (1947)
'*My Soul Praise the Lord*' (1947)
'*Prayer to the Father of Heaven*' (1948)
'*The Voice out of the Whirlwind*' (from the Book of Job) (1947)
'*O Taste and See*' (1953)
'*A Choral Flourish*' (1956)
'*A Vision of Aeroplanes*' (1956)

Principal songs for solo voice

'*Whither must I wander?*' (R.L. Stevenson) (c.1895)
'*Linden Lea*' (William Barnes) (1900)
'*Blackmore by the Stour*' (William Barnes) (c.1900)
'*The Winter's Willow*' (William Barnes) (c.1903)
'*When I am Dead* ' (Christina G. Rossetti) (1903)
The House of Life (Dante Gabriel Rossetti) (1903)
    1 '*Lovesright*'
    2 '*Silent Noon*'
    3 '*Love's Minstrels*'

    4 *'Heart's Haven'*
    5 *'Death in Love'*
    6 *'Love's Last Gift'*

Songs of Travel (R.L. Stevenson) (1905–7)

    1 *'The Vagabond'*
    2 *'Let Beauty Awake'*
    3 *'The Roadside Fire'*
    4 *'Youth and Love'*
    5 *'In Dreams'*
    6 *'The Infinite Shining Heavens'*
    7 *'Whither must I wander?'*
    8 *'Bright is the ring of words'*
    9 *'I have trod the Upward and the Downward Slope'*

On Wenlock Edge (A.E. Housman) for tenor, piano, and string quartet (1911)

    1 *'On Wenlock Edge'*
    2 *'From Far, from Eve and Morning'*
    3 *'Is my team ploughing?'*
    4 *'Oh, when I was in love with you'*
    5 *'Bredon Hill'*
    6 *'Clun'*

Four Hymns for tenor, piano, and viola obbligato (1915)

    1 *'Lord, Come Away'* (Jeremy Taylor)
    2 *'Who is that fair one?'* (Isaac Watts)
    3 *'Come Love, Come Lord'* (Richard Crashaw)
    4 *'Evening Hymn'* (Robert Bridges)

Merciless Beauty (Geoffrey Chaucer) (1922)

Four Poems by Fredegond Shove (1925)

    1 *'Motion and Stillness'*
    2 *'Four Nights'*
    3 *'The New Ghost'*
    4 *'The Water Mill'*

Two Poems by Seamus O'Sullivan (1925)

    1 *'The Twilight People'*
    2 *'A Piper'*

Three Poems by Walt Whitman (1925)

    1 *'Nocturne'*
    2 *'A Clear Midnight'*
    3 *'Joy, shipmate, Joy'*

Three Songs from Shakespeare (1925)
    1 *'Orpheus with his Lute'*
    2 *' Take, O take those lips away'*
    3 *'When icicles hang by the wall '*
In the Spring (William Barnes) (1952)
Seven Songs from 'The Pilgrim's Progress' (John Bunyan) (1952)
    1 *'Watchful's Song'*
    2 *'The Song of the Pilgrim'*
    3 *'The Pilgrim's Psalm'*
    4 *'The Song of the Leaves of Life and the Waters of Life'*
    5 *'The Song of Vanity Fair'*
    6 *'The Woodcutter's Song'*
    7 *'The Bird's Song'*
Ten Songs for Voice and Oboe (William Blake) (1958)
    1 *'Infant Joy'*
    2 *'A Poison True'*
    3 *'The Piper'*
    4 *'London'*
    5 *'The Lamb'*
    6 *'The Shepherd '*
    7 *'Ah! Sunflower'*
    8 *'Cruelty has a human heart'*
    9 *'The Divine Image'*
    10 *'Eternity*
Four Last Songs (Ursula Vaughan Williams) (pub. posth. 1960)
    1 *'Procris'*
    2 *'Tired '*
    3 *'Hands, Eyes, and Heart'*
    4 *'Menelaus'*

Arrangements for mixed voices:

Full Fathom Five (Henry Purcell) (1913)
Five English Folksongs
    1 *'The Dark-eyed Sailor'*
    2 *'The Springtime of the Year'*
    3 *'Just as the tide was flowing*
    4 *'The Lover's Ghost'*
    5 *'Wassail Song'*

'*Our Love goes out*' (1920)
'*The Lass that loves a Sailor*' (1921)
'*Heart of Oak*' (1921)
'*Loch Lomond* ' (1921)
'*The Mermaid* ' (1921)
'*Linden Lea*' (1921)
'*A Farmer's Son so sweet*' (1922)
'*Bushes and Briars*' (1924)
'*Alistair McAlpine's Lament*' (1924)
'*Ca' the Yowes*' (1924)
'*Mannin Veen*' (1924)
'*The Turtle Dove*' (1924)
'*I'll never love thee more*' (1934)
'*John Dory*' (1934)
'*Almighty Word*' (Tallis) (1953)
'*The Old Hundredth*' (1953)

Arrangements for Male Voices

'*The Jolly Ploughboy*' (1908)
'*The Winter is Gone*' (1912)
'*Down among the Dead Men*' (1912)
'*Ward the Pirate*' (1912)
'*The Turtledove*' (1912)
'*Heart of Oak*' (1921)
'*The Farmer's Boy*' (1921)
'*The Old Folks at Home*' (1921)
'*The seeds of love*' (1923)
'*High Germany*' (1923)
'*An Acre of Land*' (1933)
'*The Ploughman*' (1933)
'*The World it went well with me then*' (1935)
'*The New Commonwealth*' (1948)

EDITIONS PREPARED BY VAUGHAN WILLIAMS

Purcell's Welcome Songs: ed. for the Purcell Society in two
    volumes (1905–10)
The English Hymnal: (1906; 2nd edition 1933)

Songs of Praise: (ed. with Martin Shaw) (1925; 2nd edition 1931)
The Oxford Book of Carols: (ed. with Martin Shaw) (1928)

LITERARY WORKS OF VAUGHAN WILLIAMS

National Music (1934)
Some thoughts on Beethoven's Choral Symphony and other writings (1953)
The Making of Music (1955)

Index

CLASSIC *f*M
GARDEN PLANNER

THE GARDENING FORUM TEAM:
STEFAN BUCZACKI, FRED DOWNHAM,
SUE PHILLIPS WITH DAPHNE LEDWARD

Drawing on 125 years of collective garden experience, the formidable *Cheltenham & Gloucester Classic Gardening Forum* team of Stefan Buczacki, Fred Downham and Sue Phillips with Daphne Ledward have created a stylish planner as a companion and adviser for all your garden needs.

The authors provide practical tips on subjects ranging from growing salad leaves in spring, cultivating late colour in borders and growing herbs, to creating spectacular hanging baskets and pots. There are checklists of things to do and regular features from team members discussing favourite plants, advice on special problems, and occasionally just a few words on the delights to be enjoyed in the garden.

Throughout, there is room for the reader to make notes or journal entries, or simply to reflect on a delightful day in the garden.

£9.99   ISBN: 1 85793 964 6   Paperback

CLASSIC *f*M

MUSIC
A JOY FOR LIFE

EDWARD HEATH

Foreword by Yehudi Menuhin

Music is a record of a lifetime's passion for a subject with which former Prime Minister Sir Edward Heath has been involved since he was nine years old. In this book – first published in 1976 and now updated in his eighty-first year – Sir Edward recalls his musical experiences, from his days as a chorister in his parish church to his work as a conductor of international renown – a career that began in 1971 when he conducted the London Symphony Orchestra playing Elgar's 'Cockaigne' Overture at its gala concert in the Royal Festival Hall.

From his friendships with Herbert von Karajan and Leonard Bernstein to his great musical loves such as Beethoven and British music, from music at Downing Street to a series of five symphony concerts he conducted for his eightieth birthday celebrations, Sir Edward gives a fascinating personal insight into his wide-ranging experience. Written with great knowledge and characteristic enthusiasm, *Music – A Joy for Life* will appeal both to those who already have a serious interest in music and also to those who enjoy music and would like a greater understanding.

£16.99   ISBN: 1 86205 090 2

THE
CLASSIC *f*M
GUIDE TO
CLASSICAL MUSIC

JEREMY NICHOLAS
Consultant Editor: ROBIN RAY
Foreword by HUMPHREY BURTON

'... *a fascinating and accessible guide ... it will provide*
an informative and illuminating source of insight
for everybody from the beginner to the musicologist.'

Sir Edward Heath

The Classic fM Guide to Classical Music opens with a masterly history of classical music, illustrated with charts and lifelines, and is followed by a comprehensive guide to more than 500 composers. There are major entries detailing the lives and works of the world's most celebrated composers, as well as concise biographies of more than 300 others.

This invaluable companion to classical music combines extensive factual detail with fascinating anecdotes, and an insight into the historical and musical influences of the great composers. It also contains reviews and recommendations of the best works, and extensive cross-references to lesser-known composers. Jeremy Nicholas's vibrant, informative and carefully researched text is complemented by photographs and cartoons, and is designed for easy reference, with a comprehensive index.

£19.99   ISBN: 1 85793 760 0   Hardback
£9.99   ISBN: 1 86205 051 1   Paperback

CLASSIC *f*M
LIFELINES

With 4.8 million listeners every week, *Classic fM* is now the most listened-to national commercial radio station in the UK. With the *Classic fM Lifelines*, Pavilion Books and *Classic fM* have created an affordable series of elegantly designed short biographies that will put everyone's favourite composers into focus.

Written with enthusiasm and in a highly accessible style, the *Classic fM Lifelines* series will become the Everyman of musical biographies. Titles for the series have been chosen from *Classic fM*'s own listener surveys of the most popular composers.

£4.99 each book

CLASSIC *f*M LIFELINES

To purchase any of the books in the *Classic fM Lifelines* series
simply fill in the order form below and post or fax it,
together with your remittance, to the address below.

Please send the titles ticked below

J.S. Bach	☐	Gustav Mahler	☐
Ludwig van Beethoven	☐	Sergei Rachmaninov	☐
Johannes Brahms	☐	Franz Schubert	☐
Claude Debussy	☐	Dmitri Shostakovich	☐
Edward Elgar	☐	Pyotr Ilyich Tchaikovsky	☐
Joseph Haydn	☐	Ralph Vaughan Williams	☐

Number of titles @ £4.99 _____ Value: £_____
(carriage paid within UK)

I enclose a cheque (UK only) payable to Bookpoint ☐
OR
Please charge my credit card account ☐
I wish to pay by: Visa ☐ MasterCard ☐ Access ☐ American Express ☐

Card number | | | | | | | | | | | | | | | | |

Signature_____ Expiry Date_____
Name_____
Address_____
_____
_____ Postcode_____

Please send your order to: Marketing Department, Pavilion Books Ltd,
26 Upper Ground, London SE1 9PD, or fax for quick dispatch to:
Marketing Department, 0171-620 0042.